The Kriya Serpent Yogi

How to Transform Ordinary People into Extraordinary Humans

The Kriya Serpent Yogi

How to Transform Ordinary People into Extraordinary Humans

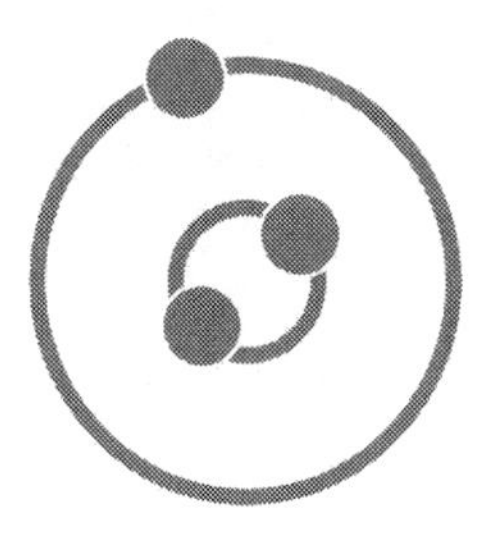

Agni Lakshya

London, UK
Washington, DC, USA

First published by Mantra Books, 2024
Mantra Books is an imprint of Collective Ink Ltd.,
Unit 11, Shepperton House, 89 Shepperton Road, London, N1 3DF
office@collectiveinkbooks.com
www.collectiveinkbooks.com
www.mantra-books.net

For distributor details and how to order please visit the 'Ordering' section on our website.

ISBN: 978 1 80341 595 6
978 1 80341 596 3 (ebook)
Library of Congress Control Number: 2023912485

A CIP catalogue record for this book is available from the British Library.

Design: Lapiz Digital Services

UK: Printed and bound by CPI Group (UK) Ltd, Croydon, CR0 4YY
Printed in North America by CPI GPS partners

We operate a distinctive and ethical publishing philosophy in all areas of our business, from our global network of authors to production and worldwide distribution.

Contents

This book is dedicated to Paramahansa Yogananda with deepest gratitude for the inspiration and promise of a greater state of living through Kriya Yoga. Were it not for his sacrifice to leave India and travel West to teach the methods and philosophies of Kriya Yoga, the West would be a much poorer place than it is today. As Humanity evolves, so too will the tools of spiritual enlightenment, but his early teachings are the foundation upon which the new humans will build.

Foreword

Welcome new humans. I know you are a new human because of your interest in this book. I want to start with a question borrowed from the HBO television series titled *Westworld* based on the novel of the same name by Michael Crichton. In the series, a theme park modeling the old American West contains characters that are robotic androids programmed with a backstory to fit the theme and their role within that theme.

These theme park characters are asked, "Have you ever questioned the nature of your reality?" They are asked this as part of an interview process before returning to the theme park after repairs that bring them back from the dead.

While the television series is superb entertainment and contains incredible insights into the ideas of freedom, free will and illusion, it isn't why I bring up this question, though there are parallels. I bring it up because I believe it is a question every new human has been asking since they were a young child. I believe the answer to this question is a resounding yes; *people question the nature of their reality!*

Today we are experiencing the dawn of new revelations that are confounding many, and it questions the nature of our reality in a very personal way. As a new human myself, I have questioned the nature of my reality my entire life, and it has led me to the creation of this book.

Between the advent of artificial intelligence, the confirmation of the God particle, and the early stages of virtual reality that will blur the lines between the real and what we think is real, humanity is on the verge of an apocryphal change. Is what you see and live everyday real or is this just another virtual reality where we are all the characters in a theme park we call earth?

Have you questioned the nature of your reality? If not, this book is probably not for you. This book represents a path for those who question reality, and that path will lead them to the true nature of reality, one that is vastly different from what they currently believe. It is the path of the Kriya Serpent Yogi. Read on new humans.

I want to take a minute to thank all the Light workers, Indigos and new humans that came before me, laying the foundations for the work I do. The work they completed will carry on through new generations of humans now manifesting on this world.

Their early efforts helped build the community and resources others, like me, used to awaken to the gestalt of reality we live in rather than the illusion most cling to. These early pioneers were derided, persecuted and called evil by the deluded humans they were tasked to awaken, and their courage and dedication are a debt we can never repay.

However, we will build off their early foundations and pave the way for the new age where all humans awaken to the true reality. Their future incarnations will awaken to a world their early efforts helped build, and they will be proud.

Thank you all for your sacrifices and willingness to put your own spiritual growth on display for all to see. You all are truly some of the Divine's greatest servants and will be blessed through the ages for your endearing and enduring work. See you on the other side!

Not only is the Universe stranger than we think,
it is stranger than we can think.
Richard P. Feynman (Physicist)

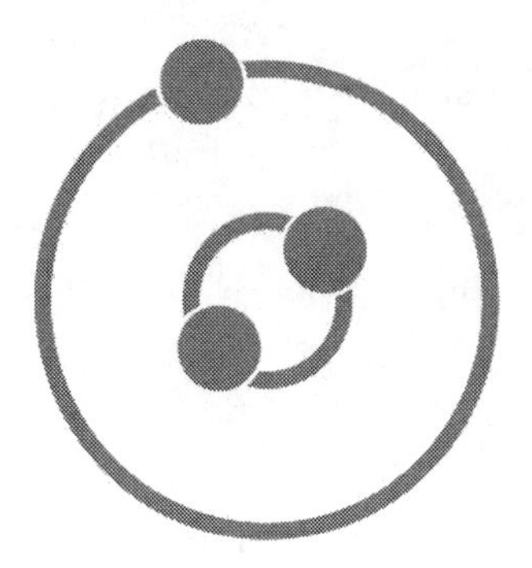

Introduction

Everything is energy, and all energy vibrates. All vibrations have frequencies. Attune your body to the frequencies, and the Universe will open up to you.

It is true. Our reality is nothing more than energy. How we perceive this energy through our senses is the illusion that fools us into believing everything is solid even though everything is not. In fact, science tells us our bodies are 99.9999999 percent empty space. All of humanity could fit within the volume of a sugar cube if the space were removed from our atoms.

Over the years, I have told my students this, and they are not sure what to do with that information. I teach them that when they touch anything they aren't actually touching matter to matter, but energy to energy. How that energy reacts with each other is what our senses perceive as touch. We are, in essence, an energetic projection similar to a hologram. In fact, all of reality we perceive with our physical senses is nothing more than a hologram, in a manner of speaking.

Think about it. A hologram is a projected image made of light. Therefore, it is only energy manifested into an image our senses perceive as something solid. Our physical senses are nothing more than energy detectors feeding data into our mind which constructs that data into something we call reality.

The concept of energy is important for many reasons. First, though many might dispute this, we possess a Soul. The Soul itself is eternal energy, as all energy is, and is currently projecting into a vessel we call our bodies, which is also just energy.

The Soul incarnates into various bodies throughout time, giving us the experiences of life in what some are now calling a *simulation*. If that means it is like some experiment, then they are correct in a manner of speaking. Our Souls create this reality simulation to permit our Souls to "experience" life and all its bumps, bruises and emotions.

There is more to the Universe and our existence than we might believe, and now is the time for new humans to learn what that is. The concept of everything being energy is one such lesson. I do not intend to bore you with theoretical physics nor ancient spiritual beliefs, but a basic understanding of a few concepts is important for you to understand the principles of why yoga works, and in particular, why Kriya Serpent Yoga can deliver some of the most amazing things I will detail within this book.

If energy is reality, and we are energy with a consciousness driving it (Soul), then learning to sense, interpret, change, and transform that energy is your key to both understanding the Universe and unlocking secrets to who you are, why you are here, and where you are going.

For thousands of years, mystics and scholars have worked tirelessly to better understand reality and our role within it.

Spiritual leaders have taught us philosophical viewpoints which indicate there is a greater consciousness that controls all that we know.

Scientists, on the other hand, have presented us with factual observations that show how all that we know works in the physical sense. Mystics have used both ends of that spectrum, spiritual and material, to better understand reality. I am a mystic, and have been at least since the advent of the Mystery Schools of Egypt.

My journey on this world has seen a multitude of lives working towards a singular purpose: *the betterment of humanity.* I am what the Buddhists call a Bodhisattva; one who works to help others find enlightenment and freedom from suffering. I practice not to achieve nirvana, unity, or any other esoteric existence but simply to help others. I love life, and being here right now doing this is *why I am here.*

Enlightenment has many levels, and I have achieved quite a few over my many incarnations. But the truth is I love the material world, and wish to manifest within it for an eternity, always helping those who need guidance. In this particular incarnation, I am here to awaken others to their purpose, so in a sense, I am a teacher first and foremost.

The goal of Kriya Serpent Yoga is not to achieve ultimate enlightenment, though it is certainly possible. Instead, its purpose is to connect you with your Soul so that you find your purpose in this incarnation to help humanity continue its evolution to its final destination: *to become creators within the Universe.* You heard me. Our destiny is to become creators, like those who have come before us (non-human).

I take my role in this process seriously, and I work tirelessly to achieve it. Humanity's evolution spans millions of years, and will likely take thousands more to achieve our vaulted status within the Cosmos. But it is an exciting journey filled with miraculous experiences, and is far more fulfilling than anything you can experience in your ordinary life. It is your purpose, and everything else pales in comparison.

I hope you begin to understand the scope of what this book contains. It is but one in a multitude of steps that will send you on a journey into the Universe to find your purpose for existing in the here and now. Previous lives will open up to you, bringing memories that will make you wiser than your years, and far more knowledgeable about the Universe and its true reality. It is not just a journey of a lifetime, but a journey of many lifetimes, each one a special step in achieving your ultimate purpose for this world.

By continuing this journey, you will evolve and grow, each incarnation a step closer to the real you, and the Divine within. We are but expressions of the great Divine, a mote in a myriad network of singular expressions. We are like neurons within a colossal brain we call the Universe. Each one is interconnected and an integral part of the whole. In this new age, we call this network Unity, and each time we reconnect with this Unity, we see each part of the whole, and understand our part in this ultimate expression of life.

This book is not a literary work, scientific journal, historical documentation of yoga, or a healthy lifestyle reference. This is a manual for those who are seeking their true spiritual purpose in this life. It purports to teach a simple yoga technique for activating the Kundalini within you so that you connect with the Divine and find your purpose.

This is a book targeted at all the new humans manifesting in this world right now. It will provide them the tools necessary to take their next evolutionary step forward in a long line of incarnations from the distant past to the current present. This step is but another diamond in a beautiful chain of your existence, each diamond brighter than the one before.

Are you a new human? If so, this book is for you. Not sure? Then continue onward, and I will help you discover the truth for yourself. This is a book of awakenings; your awakening. I have already awakened to my purpose, and this book is a product of that. What will be yours? If you never take that first step, you may never know.

Knowing is what this is all about. Belief is well and good, and it has served humanity for thousands of years, but that time is ending. Now is the time for us to *experience* reality, not just believe in it. Once you finally experience it, you can never go back, nor would you want to.

You see, all of us, in each incarnation, are born into this reality with knowledge of our true self. But the process of growing and evolving within the world of our senses creates a veil that hides this reality from us. I still have very young memories (a year or so) where I knew where I came from and all those who were there with me before. But the veil of life grew over my spiritual eye, hiding that reality. When I have told people about these early memories, they say it was nothing more than childish imagination running wild.

And that is how the veil is created. We are indoctrinated with it through the dogmatic knowledge inflicted upon us from a very young age. Science tells us there is nothing beyond that which we can sense with our physical bodies. Religion tells us there is so much more, but that we are denied it because of sin, or evil, or some other reasons, and our only hope in reaching these non-physical realities is through belief and religious doctrine. They claim we cannot achieve it by ourselves.

That is utter *nonsense*. We all are an expression of the Divine, therefore we have access to the powers of the Divine, and once we brush away the veil that hides reality from us, we can begin to use those powers to create the reality we want. Be careful, because what you think you may want may not be what you really want. It all comes down to the *real* you (Soul) against the *illusion* of you (ego).

Only the Soul knows what you really are and what you really want, so until you reconnect with that ethereal part of you, the ego is in control, spinning the web of illusion just as it was indoctrinated to do. In Buddhist traditions, we call the mind the ego.

Before we get too far, I want to make something abundantly clear. This book is designed to provide new humans with new tools that will help them connect with their Soul (Divine), detach from the illusion of their ego, find their true purpose, and begin an amazing incarnation traveling down the path of that purpose. I offer nothing else but the truth.

If you come seeking answers to the esoteric questions of existentiality, I will direct you to the Divine, for that is where those answers lie. I am not your guru. I am not your leader. I am not your soothsayer, philosopher, father figure, or any other person of significant influence in your life. I am a teacher that will give you the tools to find yourself so that you will never need all those other people. You will be your own master, and you will experience the truth of things, and once you have, you will never be the same.

In this moment of humanity's history, we are at the dawn of the age of the individual. *Awaken them, and they shall find the path on their own*. The only guide you will need is the Divine within. But first, you must awaken to who you truly are.

There is a lot to unpack here, and you would be wise to question everything. Belief is not enough. One must *know* rather than believe. To *experience* and to actually *know* is the goal. Only then, can you grow into that which you were destined to become, because that is everyone's role in each incarnation, to experience and evolve.

Then you will *know*, and you will never question the true nature of reality again. You will never fear death, you will never have anxiety about living, and you will relish each day as though it is a gift, for that is why it is called the present.

I want to take a few paragraphs to acknowledge the efforts of those before me. This book is not intended to be a replacement of the teachings that have come before. All teachings, but especially yogic teachings are valuable assets to all of humanity. Kriya Yoga is a miraculous tool we can use to achieve incredible spiritual growth, and it would be wrong for anyone to believe those other teachings cannot achieve similar or identical results.

Kriya Serpent Yoga is an extension to those existing techniques, but those existing techniques still provide remarkable benefits. In fact, you will see in this book many of those techniques which are foundational to the preparation and use of the Kriya Serpent techniques I present. While there will be many critics when it comes to Kriya Serpent Yoga, I will ask you to ignore them and make your own decision based on your own experiences.

There is no judgment here about any spiritual practice, yoga or otherwise. To deny anyone the opportunity to spiritually grow and flourish because of some sense of purity, dogma, or beliefs is, in a sense, the root of all evil. Think about how many wars have been fought over religious differences. When we impose our own beliefs and desires on others, we are traveling down the path of delusion. It is nothing more than blind hubris to expect all others in the world to believe as you do, practice as you do and live as you do.

We are here to experience all that life can be, and that includes all spiritual practices. We need not try them all, but when we find one that works for us and our needs, we must respect the choices others have made even if it is very different from our own. *Free will* is a Universal Law, and to deny that from a spiritual standpoint is to deny the very fabric of our reality.

I want to thank Lahiri Mahasaya for bringing Kriya Yoga back into the world for all to benefit. I want to thank Paramahansa Yogananda for delivering those teachings from India to America. I want to thank all those who have taught, practiced and spread the knowledge of Kriya Yoga throughout the world. Your efforts have brought humanity closer to the dawn of the new age of the new humans.

I want to thank J.C. Stevens for his book *Kriya Secrets Revealed* for bringing Kriya Yoga into the world for all who can read. His instructions are certainly an inspiration for my own practice as well as for this book. Likewise, I want to thank Santata Gamana for all his books about Kriya Yoga and other spiritual practices. I learned a great deal from his teachings, and use his books as references when needed.

In particular, *Kriya Yoga Exposed* was instrumental in re-starting me down the Kriya Yoga path. His books are a must read for anyone's spiritual library for you will learn something new and valuable from each and every one.

Before I end this introduction, I will impart one more lesson. If energy is everything, and we swim within a Universe filled with energy, then interacting with that energy is not only possible but unavoidable.

If our thoughts are merely energy generated within our brains, then transmitting and receiving that energy (thoughts) should also be possible. Carrying that assumption forward, manipulating other energy using transmitted thoughts surely must be possible, assuming we learn the techniques to make that happen.

In fact, if our bodies are nothing more than a holographic manifestation of our Souls within the energy Ocean we call the Universe then learning to manifest other holographic things should also be possible assuming we learn to harness that inherent power within our Souls.

This is not just speculation, but the natural laws within our holographic Universe. It means that things such as telepathy, telekinesis, clairvoyance, remote healing, astral projection, and remote viewing are all possible, as each is simply a manipulation of energy which everything we call our reality is made of. *Consciousness* is the key, and therein we find our *Soul*.

Now, this doesn't mean this book is about learning those things. It is about connecting you with your Soul in a real way and learning about its manifestation in the physical plane which is you. You will not learn about the Noetic Sciences within these pages, but when you begin to master Kriya Serpent Yoga, the Noetic Sciences will begin to manifest within you.

We all have potential, but most are not connected with their Souls and cannot manifest that potential. Are you ready to fully experience the reality of this Universe? Move onward!

Chapter 1

I think, therefore I am.
Rene Descartes

Who Am I?

It makes perfect sense to ask why you need another yoga book. You can find everything you need to enhance your life and spirituality within the myriad volumes of yoga books and websites available today. But ask yourself this question: *Why am I here?* This is the penultimate existential question. Want the answer?

First, who am I, Agni Lakshya? I am not a yogi from India, though I have taken a pen name in Sanskrit. I am not a spiritual leader building a flock of followers to change the world, though change the world we will. Like you, I am just an ordinary person from an ordinary background but awakened.

I was born into a middle class family in the suburbs of the United States of America, and went through public education within a conservative religious family. Yes, I was raised Christian, but don't hold that against me or credit me for it. Though it played a role in my early spiritual education, there was something about traditional Christianity that never quite fit. So, like many others, I went in search of answers.

While searching the vaulted halls of science, I learned as much as I could, trying to piece together a view of our great Universe from a plethora of rational thinking that often denied intelligent design in favor of random chance.

Despite this science background, I dabbled in the exploration of the paranormal, predominantly because of my experiences with it. My partner once said, "You can't un-see it!" It is true; you cannot un-see it and therefore must pursue an understanding of it.

But even with all this information, I was attempting to force it into an ancient paradigm into which I'd been indoctrinated. It was the Judeo-Christian paradigm, and it left me wanting. So I did what many do and sank into the deepest depths of materialism and hedonism, searching for answers through the exultation of the physical senses. It was a selfish act, and though I often look back with a sense of shame, I have to be honest with myself and admit I liked it. But the answers didn't come, and neither did genuine happiness.

There is a philosophical belief that one must fall hard before they can truly rise spiritually, and I suppose for me that is true. After twenty wonderful years together, I lost the love of my life, my Soulmate, to cancer.

The loss devastated me and left me with two young daughters depending on me as their sole provider and parental figure. I did what many do and fell apart in despair and alcohol abuse. I hit the proverbial *rock bottom*.

Now, before you get concerned, my daughters are perfectly fine and are the most amazing young women I have been blessed to know. And I have known a lot because I am also a teacher of high school mathematics. Did I not mention that? Well, let's rewind a bit and look at my professional and educational achievements before we return to rock bottom.

After graduating from high school with a science bent, I enlisted in the US Army and served four years as a radio and radio-teletype operator in the Infantry. Based on my early field promotion to Sergeant, it was clear my talents were better suited elsewhere.

After leaving the military, I attended the University of Colorado studying Electrical Engineering. It was a fascinating field, though very rigorous. Along the way, I discovered I had a strong aptitude for technology and more specifically, programming. With that epiphany, I switched my major to Computer Science and applied my natural talents to writing software for computer systems.

I graduated with a Bachelor of Science in Computer Science and went straight into telecommunications, writing software for early email and telephony systems. Software was my niche, and I imagined, as many did, that I would someday be a powerful technologist similar to a Bill Gates or a Mark Zuckerberg for you younger crowds. That was not to be, though I did work at Microsoft at one point.

It was during this post-university timeframe that I married my wonderful wife whose belief system was what one might call New Age. She had several spiritual experiences during a Native American drum circle in Montana that changed her view of the Universe and awakened something within her. It awakened memories of past lives. When she shared these beliefs with me, I did not know what to make of them as I did not believe in reincarnation. She held on to those beliefs unto the end.

Several years into our marriage, she began discussing my incessant observations about the broken world that needed serious renovation. She told me point blank that I was what is known as an *Indigo Child,* a more spiritually advanced human sent here during the dawn of the new age of humanity that was coming. New Age folk know that as the dawning of the *Age of Aquarius*. Hmmm... I am Aquarius.

Okay, I'll admit, though I found it all fascinating, I was skeptical at best, and completely against such concepts at worst. After all, I was a software engineer addicted to science and technology. I saw the future and it was not full of mystical nonsense and ancient mysteries about a new age. The new age I saw was artificial intelligence, robots, genetics and space travel, duh! I had read the *Foundation* and *Dune* series; I knew what the future held.

Though I have since discovered those things will actually play a large role in our future, I do not wish to digress into that discussion within this book. There was a problem with my myopic view of the Universe. I'd had so many mystical experiences throughout my life and never once reconciled those experiences with my religious background or my fundamental education in science and rational thinking.

And there it was. I was deeply immersed in a foundation of three very different views of the Universe and couldn't resolve the discrepancies. My wife knew of my conundrum, but was exasperated by my unwillingness to travel her New Age path. She never succeeded in waking me up until after she passed away.

I still didn't believe in reincarnation and questioned the existence of God, Jesus, Angels and anything that smacked of hoodoo voodoo. This forced me to turn my back against the reality of the ghostly and psychic experiences I'd had throughout my life so I could embrace the cold hard world without spirituality and only the things we can measure and reproduce. I was a victim of a left-brained education system, where all that mattered was rational thought.

Spirituality? I'll be honest; I kind of viewed it as a joke. These were foolish people clinging to ancient beliefs that let our ancestors sleep at night when life was scary and full of terrors. The rational person was enlightened through the art of sciences and well beyond those ancient mythical beliefs. We would create our own world, our own heaven and solve all the problems with technology and knowledge. We didn't need ancient, invisible agents helping us. If anything, they were holding us back. I didn't tell my wife all of this, but it was what I was thinking.

So, some of you might think, paranormal, huh? What could be so persuasive to pique his curiosity about that? Well, here are my experiences: Premonitions, Disembodied Entities, Religious Experiences, Telepathy and Psychic attacks. I will let you take that as you will.

Now imagine a man of science having to deal with all those types of experiences. Yes, *personal* experiences! It made no sense to me, but I figured that somewhere there had to be some rational scientific theory or property of the Universe that would explain it all. Turns out I was right, and I was also very wrong.

The world does not like the paranormal for the following reasons. From a religious standpoint, most consider it dabbling in black magic or satanic arts. Therefore, no one in the religious communities will touch it unless you are looking for an exorcism.

The paranormal does not fit into the scientific community either, since it deviates from existing theories and rational understandings of how our Universe works. Therefore, it is shunned by most of the scientific and academic communities as anathema and anyone careless enough to investigate it is ostracized. *So much for the frontiers of science.*

All of this put me in a difficult position regarding my own experiences. I could deny my own experiences and adhere to either of the "accepted" views of the Universe or continue my search, hoping something might come along that would make it all fit together. I wasn't wrong, something came along... *rock bottom.*

Now, some of you might think, damn, that same stuff has happened to me. New humans are popping up all over the world, and their experiences do not always mesh with the way they are educated. In fact, for most of them, they feel like they were dropped off onto the wrong planet. I have felt that way my whole life.

If that is you, bear with me as I lay out some fundamental thinking that might bring clarity to your existence. But first, back to rock bottom. Yes, the grief of my loss had placed me in a tailspin, and things were looking grim, despite being responsible for these two young girls. Fear not, things took a turn.

After a twelve-year career in technology, I was forced out during the 2000 Dot Com crash. For those who are not old enough to remember, that technology crash permanently wiped out at least one third of the talented engineers in the USA. I was one of them, and I was forced to change tracks to support my family. Since I had always wanted to write novels, I decided to switch into teaching. My goal was to teach technology and computer science at the secondary level, so I acquired a master's degree from my alma mater, the University of Colorado, and began my teaching career teaching mathematics to high school students.

It was shortly after I began teaching that I started writing novels, and my wife and I decided to have children. At this point, we had been together for twelve years, and it was an amazing marriage. We were still madly in love with each other, and bringing children into our lives would be the icing on the proverbial cake. And it truly was, until my wife discovered an unusual sore on her tongue during a routine visit to the dentist!

Let me rewind a bit. A year before she was diagnosed and a few months after our second daughter was born, I was taking a shower during one fine summer morning. As I stepped into the warm water, I was suddenly gripped by an intense vision. In it, I was utterly alone, raising my children without my wife who had passed away. In this vision, I saw her funeral, my two daughters standing beside me in tears as I held a black rose in my hand. It was so powerful, I nearly dropped to the shower floor but leaned heavily against the wall as tears streamed down my face.

I had experienced yet another premonition of someone's death, and this time it was my wife's. I was shaken by the experience, but never told my wife or anyone else until she had passed away. It was another paranormal experience I could not fit into my rational world. She passed away nearly four years later after fighting a brutal battle against cancer for three years

When she died, my wife and I had been together for twenty years, and losing her was one of the most difficult things I had ever experienced in my life. Our daughters were five and four when at that time, and for a brief while afterwards, I cried often, triggered by the most mundane things. I drank so heavily that I could barely wake up in the mornings, and my attitude about everything was overly cynical. I even had thoughts of suicide. Welcome to *rock bottom*.

That is when my wife *visited me* while I was watching a show about the life of the recently deceased Steve Jobs, co-founder of Apple. I was already into my second martini when the show mentioned Steve's life as a devout Buddhist. At that very moment, I felt my wife's spirit merge with mine, and her voice spoke crystal clear in my mind, telling me I had to study Buddhism. I knew my wife almost as well as I knew myself, and I knew her voice and the feeling of her spirit. She was setting me on a path of healing.

I broke down and poured my drink out as I realized she was trying to save me from beyond the grave. How could she do that? Don't we just die and disappear forever? How could she speak to me from beyond? What was beyond? This time, I didn't turn away and disregard the experience. This time, I did as she asked and learned everything I could about Buddhism.

Now here is where it gets really interesting. As I started studying Buddhism, I had this uncanny Déjà vu that I was actually *re-learning* it. It was as though I already knew about it. I had never studied it, yet it resonated with me like an old friend. It was like I already believed in it, even though I had never read, seen, or heard anything about it in my whole life.

Keep in mind, I still didn't believe in reincarnation, even though my wife had. She always claimed to have memories of her past lives, but I didn't believe her because I didn't have any of those same memories. Not yet.

For ten years after my wife's death, I studied everything I could about Buddhism. I tried various flavors, searching for one that fit. I tried Japanese Nicheren Daishonin Buddhism and liked a lot of things about it. Chanting *Nam Myoho Renge Kyo* made me feel better and see the world through compassionate eyes. I tried Zen and learned to still my mind of all thoughts and sit in silence.

Then one day, I was reading an interview with someone in a Buddhist publication and saw they mentioned a book called *Autobiography of a Yogi*. It had made a tremendous impact on their life and Buddhist practice. Intrigued, I bought the e-book edition of it. Reading that book was a profound experience. *The first of many yet to come*. My Soul was stirring from slumber.

If you haven't already, I recommend reading this book. It moved me in a way I had never experienced before, and I soon joined the Self Realization Fellowship (SRF) founded by the Yogi, Paramahansa Yogananda, whose autobiography I had just read. I wanted to learn what he offered, and I went through the year-long lessons, following them to the letter. My mind calmed, my disposition became happy, and I felt an incredible peace.

Eight months into the course, I was sleeping in my room, my dog on the floor as usual. Back then, I kept my door open to allow me to hear my children when they came out to the kitchen for a drink, or to let me know when they were sick, or to ask to sleep in my bed when scared. My sleep back then was rather light. I heard something outside my room, and my dog woke up since she'd heard it, too.

I sat up in bed and looked out the door, expecting one of my children to appear in the doorway. Instead, a dazzling, golden light appeared, illuminating my entire room in warm sunshine. Within the golden light was the figure of Paramahansa Yogananda adorned in golden silk robes gilded with sparkling gems. It blew away me and tears streamed down my face as I felt a radiating love from his smiling face. It lasted only a couple minutes, but the profound nature of it was incredulous.

When the light and his image finally faded, I felt a loving embrace within the depths of my Soul. My dog, having experienced the same thing, walked to the doorway and looked all over for the Yogi before returning to bed. I was seriously moved by such a profound experience. It was nearly identical to the experiences Paramahansa Yogananda had written about in his autobiography.

I finished the introductory course with the SRF, but was forced to stop when I could not make a serious commitment as a single parent with two young girls. I was angry because I had done everything they had instructed me to and experienced such a joyful moment when the Yogi visited me, but I could not continue the studies without a commitment.

I stopped pursuing the Kriya Yoga path, stymied. It was an enormous disappointment in my life. Then, I started dating and became lost in the real world before turning back down the Zen path. Eventually, I found myself back with the first Buddhism I had practiced: the Buddhism of the Soka Gakkai International (SGI).

The Soka Gakkai International is a wonderful organization founded on the teachings of Nicheren Daishonin. It teaches us about the transformation of all humans through a simple meditation practice based on the Lotus Sutra. I joined the local organization and am still a member, in name at least, if not in practice. But despite the fantastic community and wonderful feelings from the practice, something gnawed at me.

When the Covid-19 pandemic began in early 2020, I was once again a bit of a lost Soul. My meditation practice fell off, and I returned to old habits while developing new ones. All of them were designed to distract me from the fact that I was an unhappy person. I struggled at work, personally and spiritually.

Bouts of depression became commonplace, mostly because of an increase in drinking and gaming online. Yeah, I was addicted to *Fortnite* and *Apex Legends*. I was very good at both and spent far too many hours of my life playing them. It was an unwholesome waste of my life.

When the pandemic hit, all the gyms closed, so now I was gaming, eating, drinking, and gained over twenty-five pounds within a month. I was on a destructive path like so many of us during those early months of the pandemic. I saw my end looming in the distance.

At the end of May 2020, I was in the worst shape I had ever been in since my wife had died. I looked in the mirror one morning, disgusted with the person staring back at me. I was overweight, pasty white with dark bags under my eyes. Rock meets bottom once again. At that moment, I vowed to change everything and start down a healthier path.

Part of this new me vowed to embrace my spiritual, supernatural, and paranormal experiences in ways I never really had before. I sought everything I could about ESP, or what I now know as the Noetic Sciences. I learned of an app through one book and trained myself to hone and develop my psi abilities. It worked.

I read as much as I could on the paranormal, attempting to find a commonality between various experiences. And I did. There was the concept of energy and manifesting, which I found fascinating. Whether these entities were spirits of long dead humans or something entirely different, well, my jury is still out on that, but I realized energy has an intelligence that can manifest in the real world from what might be termed another dimension of reality.

This led me to a fascination with extraterrestrials and their role in the development and evolution of our world. Patterns emerged from all that information, and that led me to Dr. Steven Greer and his CE-5 Contact Protocol.

I tried it out at home, and things happened. Instead of turning away as I had in my past, I embraced it and dug deeper, trying to peer beyond the veil of worlds, dimensions and states of consciousness. But despite all these things I experienced and learned, something fundamental was missing, but I didn't know what.

In December 2020, I was reading more material from Dr. Greer, and he was talking about meditation and deeper states of consciousness necessary to make contact. He was a devout practitioner of meditation, and though I was back to my earlier work in the SRF, I was making little to no forward progress.

I was frustrated and finally searched feverishly on the Internet to find anything about the advanced lessons of Kriya Yoga. That is when I found Santata Gamana, a former SRF member who'd also become frustrated and revealed the secrets of Kriya Yoga guarded for so long by the masters and yogis.

This was essential knowledge to human evolution, and many were guarding it as though only a select few could ever attain benefit from it. I believe the SRF had fallen into the trap of regimented dogma. Today, you can find a lot of information on Kriya Yoga with a simple search. I am not trying to disparage the SRF, their mission is still noble, but new humans no longer need such organizations to attain spiritual enlightenment.

I get it. The yogi and disciple are a foundational piece of the Kriya Yoga history, so why wouldn't they continue this practice? Well, they don't have knowledge some of us have:

the world needs this now! After I began learning the advanced methods, I immediately began to experience Kundalini, and it changed me dramatically. It was the missing ingredient to my spiritual journey—that transcendental state needed to contact the Divine within.

A month after beginning a daily practice of Kriya Yoga, my Kundalini surged during my meditation for the first time. The rush of energy from my Base chakra to my Third Eye was so intense that it scared me. I felt taken up in a whirlwind of energy that changed my state of consciousness, and then it happened. I felt myself break apart into a million pieces, all being swept away in the energy as they merged with the infinite. *I panicked!*

I didn't know what was happening, but it felt like I was being disintegrated into nothingness. I pulled everything back into me and came out of my deep meditative state. Only later did I learn I was experiencing Samadhi, a merging with unity. When I found that out, I was so angry that fear caused me to miss that incredible experience. I have never achieved it again, yet.

Kriya Yoga delivered every promise Paramahansa Yogananda had written about in his autobiography. I dug into even more material and explored new areas such as Tantric Yoga. I integrated Bandhas into my practice, and my Kundalini was rewarding my efforts as energy surged through my body and mind, taking me to incredible states of consciousness and experiences. But there was a downside.

The body and mind are not always prepared for the intensity of Kundalini when exposed so quickly, and that has consequences. Anxiety was the biggest effect, but occasional nightmares that woke me in terror were common. I wasn't grounding myself properly and pushed myself too hard. When I learned something new in my meditation, I read about it later in one of my books. I was insatiable.

How did I know this stuff before I had read about it? A voice had emerged, and it instructed me on the methods and pacing before I learned about it in the books. In these transcendental states, I had an internal yogi training me.

As it turns out, this is the new model for learning advanced transcendental meditation. Before, you had to seek an ashram and train with a yogi, but now, those masters can speak to us through our meditation. They are waiting to train all the *new humans*.

It didn't take long before I was learning all about the ages of humanity and the enlightenment of all humans to the reality of the Universe and our role and purpose within it.

We are not helpless beings waiting for some deity to rescue us. We have all the powers of the Divine, and the *new humans*, or what I am calling Homo illustratus (the awakened ones), will be the ones finally equipped to embrace and use this Divine power through the guidance of the connection established through transcendental meditation.

How do I know this? Simple. The Divine gave me my purpose and the tools to carry it out. This incredible revelation came to me while I was driving through the Arizona desert on my way back from a trip to Phoenix. Suddenly, a vision flooded my mind and with it the commands to carry out this vision in this lifetime.

In this vision, I was to awaken as many of the new humans as possible through transcendental meditation, and engage them in the design of the new world as the old one crumbles and passes into history. This writing is part of that purpose: *to awaken the new humans*.

"Hello, wake up!"

Okay, not necessarily that easy, but not necessarily that much harder either. We'll get to that.

First, I will digress back to my wife. She always told me I was here to help usher in the new age. She didn't know how, but she knew I was an Indigo Child and this was my purpose in this lifetime. Boy, she wasn't wrong. I have since learned about some people who are nothing more than messengers for those of us who must awaken. I believe my wife was a messenger sent to tell me to look inward and find my purpose.

Most *new humans* are equipped to handle the intense energy of Kundalini and will not require decades of practice in the arts of meditation within a monastery, ashram, or any other organization dedicated to such purposes. They will have guidance from within, simple meditation techniques to stimulate the Kundalini, and the ability to connect with the Divine to discover their purpose and how to achieve it. There will be a community of like-minded humans ready to help each other manifest this new world.

See, here is the difference between the old age and the new age. In the old age, it was all about total enlightenment, a disconnection from the real world in favor of another world within the Unity of the Universal Consciousness. Sure, that all sounds great, but what if you really love life in the physical plane?

Today, it is all about energy, knowledge, and psi abilities to build a new world here in the "real." We embrace life with all its pains, complexities, and diversions as part of our continuing evolutionary process, while growing the part of us that most needs evolving: *our spirituality.*

Along the way, we will experience new vistas, learn more about our past and future, and be part of an ever growing Universe we will soon understand. It is a Universe of diversity we are only beginning to fully comprehend. We will have help from more enlightened beings ready to teach us those early steps into this new frontier.

This book is but a stepping stone on the way to this new world we will build together. If you are already engaged in your purpose, then, no need to proceed in this book except out of intellectual curiosity. However, if you believe you might be a *new human* looking for a connection to the Divine to learn your purpose, then *Kriya Serpent Yoga* is the gateway to that new path.

Kriya Serpent Yoga is just a variation of Kriya Yoga that integrates existing techniques with new ones to connect you with the Divine in very little time. You will learn simple daily practices and be rewarded with immense progress which will keep you dedicated to your journey. Read on to find this path on your grand journey into a new realm of human existence. Don't you want an answer to that existential question? Why are you here?

So, who am I? I am an ancient Soul who has been a demigod, a king, an initiate of the Egyptian School of Mysteries, a peasant, a shaman, a Templar Knight, a soldier, an engineer, a teacher, a mystic and now a Kriya Serpent Yogi.

In each of these incarnations, I have traveled a spiritual journey of evolution and purpose. I am here at the cusp of this new Age of Aquarius to once again serve the Divine for the betterment of humanity. This book and the yoga within its pages are my contributions to my purpose to wake those other ancient Souls so we can work together once more.

Join me in our quest to help humanity rise into the heavens as noble beings of light and love. If you are a new human, then you are an ancient Soul being called again to service. Become a Kriya Serpent Yogi to remake this world into the home we all deserve. It is your reason for being here at this pivotal time in human history.

Chapter 2

It is paradoxical, yet true, to say, that the more we know, the more ignorant we become in the absolute sense, for it is only through enlightenment that we become conscious of our limitations. Precisely one of the most gratifying results of intellectual evolution is the continuous opening up of new and greater prospects.
Nikola Tesla

Who Are the New Humans?

Are you a new human? Am I a new human? What is a new human? Well, like all evolutionary tales, a time comes when the newer generations are better than their predecessors. Often, this incremental change is small and cumulative over long timeframes, but at other times, it can be extreme and rather fast.

I am not an evolutionary scientist, but I understand the basic principles at work. When environmental challenges occur, some genetic mutations become more favored over others. In these situations, those mutations overcome the environmental challenges thus favoring the production of progeny to carry the mutation forward into subsequent generations. This transforms the mutation into the norm rather than the exception.

I always tell my students they are better versions than their parents, from a genetic standpoint. What I mean by that is each subsequent generation produces more favored individuals to carry specific mutations forward than the previous generations. Unfortunately, this is often skewed by interventions in the natural selection process through technology and communal intercession. In these cases, the results can produce unwanted mutations that are propagated into future generations causing disease and maladies.

Now, imagine at some point the introduction of mutations into the species resulted from genetic manipulation. Since we do not currently support the legal modification of DNA in humans, then natural selection would have to play a major role in any future changes to that species. So where does that leave us?

A more advanced species re-engineered humans in the distant past and built instructions into our DNA that, when activated, resulted in an exponential leap forward in our capabilities. They designed these capabilities to manifest when the species developed a certain level of technological progress so our species could move forward by developing the mental and physical capacities to handle the complex, ever-changing landscape of our exponential technological innovations.

This is not fantasy, but an inherent reality of our species. We were engineered to develop into the sentient, intellectual and spiritual beings we are today. The next phase of our engineered DNA is activating now since we have achieved a sufficient technological level. The exponential leap in our technology was not random.

Proper environmental conditions existed to activate our DNA. The advent of radio and our eventual immersion into this flow of electromagnetic radiation activated our DNA to begin our ascension into a technological future as spiritual entities with newfound abilities.

Remember, I said we are essentially energy. Radio waves, or electromagnetic radiation (aka light), interacted with our energy fields, causing the activation of our DNA. There is a specific range or combination of frequencies that was programmed into our DNA. The modern day radio wave pollution signaled the technological progress of our species, thus starting the process.

Now, I do not expect many people to believe this, and it doesn't really matter if you do, but the truth is, we are changing in response to our evolutionary destiny pre-ordained to trigger when we were sufficiently advanced enough to produce radio wave technology.

Think about the past 100 years. What has happened since we made the world smaller through radio? Technological explosions and enormous cultural shifts began shortly after we invented the radio and its myriad forms of communication. It triggered our DNA, ushering in the beginning of the new age of humanity.

So, who are these new humans? I call them Homo illustratus, or the *Enlightened Ones*. We know them by many other names, including Indigos, Light workers, Psychics, Mediums, Spiritualists, New Agers, Mystics, among others. They were waiting for the advent of this new age, where they would manifest in large numbers to help humanity through the transition.

They are a better version of Homo sapiens sapiens. From here on out, I will simply refer to them as Homo sapiens. Homo sapiens have persisted for a long time, and their place in history is quite storied. But their time has passed and they will soon be wiped away by the sands of time. They will persist for a while yet, but their numbers will continually dwindle as more Homo illustratus incarnate into this world.

As a high school teacher, I have seen it happening in my classrooms. These new humans are often odd students that don't quite fit in with everyone else. They are confused by the cultures and systems they must adhere to, and they often suffer from debilitating mental health issues like depression, anxiety, and panic attacks. They are confused.

Some of them fall within the Autism spectrum and often display anti-social behavior. But if you befriend one, they can be fiercely loyal to a fault. They talk about a future world where things are different, commenting on nearly everything they see as broken in the current world. They are not wrong.

Many of them exhibit incredible intuition and other psychic abilities but suppress them because of a world that shuns such gifts or demonizes them. They do not speak of it because they have had too many Homo sapiens tell them they are crazy. All new humans know what I am talking about.

A lot of these new humans immerse themselves in technology, finding comfort with electronics and software. Others become engineers, developing a passion to fix broken things. These new humans are the first to pierce the illusions and lies spun by Homo sapiens and too often turn away from the political process because of what they see.

It is hard for most to imagine such people will have such an enormous impact on humanity and this world, but they will. But first, they have to learn about their true identity and train to take over when the old world crumbles around them. They must learn the truth of things and manifest their past life memories and psychic abilities. Only then will they begin to make a significant impact. That is where Kriya Serpent Yoga comes in.

The new humans are highly advanced in the following main areas, which will make them stand out from Homo sapiens: Physical, Intellectual, Creative and Spiritual. We already see much of the physical prowess manifesting in adrenaline junkies who continue to bend the laws of physical limits. They will be our explorers through space and new worlds.

Those who have strong intellectual capacity will develop exponential leaps in innovation, science and engineering. What once seemed impossible will quickly become an everyday part of our culture and society. Many of them are already here but gobbled up by greedy corporate interests or governments that fear repercussions from their new technologies. These governments are not necessarily misguided.

The creative new humans will lead cultural shifts through art and lifestyles. They are already making these changes as influencers across the Internet, but many are not connected to the Divine, so they shift the world towards a more selfish, hedonistic lifestyle rather than altruism. They are still trapped within the illusions of Homo sapiens. That will change when they discover their Soul and connect to the Divine within.

The spiritually gifted humans will be leaders, guides and enablers of the new age. They will establish global connections to the Divine and introduce humanity to our galactic neighbors. They will manage increased human psychic abilities and establish moral and ethical codes to deal with these manifestations.

In fact, they will begin the manifestation of our new world and teach everyone else how to take part in this transformation. They will be teachers, ambassadors and, for lack of a better term, spiritual advisors. Working with their peers, they will reshape our world into the world we were meant to inherit.

Homo illustratus will grab the reins of humanity and forge a world of technological wonder through spiritual wisdom. Current misconceptions within religion will disappear as everyone is connected to the Divine within. Archaic notions of race, gender and nationality will perish as we welcome a Universe teeming with diversity.

Homo illustratus would not put the planet at risk for the benefit of a few individuals. On the other hand, Homo sapiens not only support benefitting a few at the expense of the many, but promote it as logical and practical, killing off the majority in favor of the minority. It is absurd and only eclipsed by the ridiculous concept of calling it our birthright. They are lazy and have no interest in doing what is right for the collective. They are stuck in the *survival of the fittest* mentality of animals. We did not come this far to live like animals.

Humans did not create this planet, and have no right to destroy it. In fact, it was gifted to us and is our responsibility to take care of it. Life is precious, because the conditions to support life in the Universe are the exception. To consider destroying this precious commodity is the pinnacle of absurdity, so shame on us for continuing to support this.

Yes, we are all guilty, even the new humans. But that is because we were all raised and indoctrinated in the school of Homo sapiens, where power and riches are more important than life. So how do we un-indoctrinate ourselves? *Kriya Serpent Yoga*. Connect with the Divine, realize the futility of the current path of Homo sapiens, and you will quickly re-orient to the proper viewpoint.

Homo sapiens will perish, otherwise all of humanity will. Their hubris is outlandish, unchecked and an example of what happens when you allow a species to run amok with nothing to rein it in. The only predators for Homo sapiens are global disasters and Homo sapiens.

While war and disease kept us in check for a long time, we now possess the weapons to destroy all life on this planet. Think about that for one moment, and I mean really think about it. *How stupid and ridiculous!* It is the proverbial cut off your nose to spite your face. Humans are now our own worst enemies, and this entire circus of self-annihilation is run by, you guessed it, Homo sapiens.

In a way, we cannot blame them. In the last 120 years, we had two world wars, each killing countless millions in the name of leaders whose greed and hubris could not be checked. Survival for the common person in the early 1900s was appalling, and the death of children during that unenlightened age was staggering.

During World War II, the stakes were so high it required the creation of the most horrifying weaponry ever conceived just to win the war. It was frightening and terrified the entire planet with its destructive power. They won, but didn't know what to do after that.

Those Homo sapiens had been conditioned by their experiences to fear everything and never permit deviation from established norms. Remember the communist "witch-hunt" in the 1950s in the USA? I truly get it; they were classically conditioned to act like cornered animals. However, their time is over, and they must move on.

They will perish because our species must survive, and Homo illustratus will rise from their ashes to re-create the world the way it should be, without stupidity, greed and reckless abandon while ignoring the very Divine nature we have been endowed with. Homo sapiens claim allegiance to God and then turn around and curse God under their breaths.

Our technology is rapidly outpacing our ability to control it with the archaic structures and processes developed before radio was even invented. They cling to the past with increasing frequency, searching for answers in the dusty tomes of humanity rather than the shining wisdom of those who have been within this Universe for billions of years before we were a dream.

If we turn to them, we can learn how to guide our species through these incredibly complex and challenging growing pains as we develop new technologies that use the very underpinnings of the Universe itself.

No more hubris! We must admit we are not ready for such responsibility and make the necessary changes to adapt or we shall perish. This is not a threat, but a certainty if we continue down the path of Homo sapiens. I have been shown that future, and it is total planetary destruction.

So why are Homo illutratus better than Homo sapiens in this new age? They have the accumulated memories of countless lifetimes while pursuing the emergence of humanity onto the Universal stage. Their DNA is activating incredible physical, mental and psychic abilities that allow them to see the Universe and technology in a way Homo sapiens cannot.

Ancient Souls are re-incarnating into these new humans to carry knowledge forward and resurface memories of previous lifetimes that span billions of years and worlds they helped evolve. I am one of those Souls, and I have been doing this work for over a billion years on countless worlds.

At the deepest level of my Soul, I am truly an engineer and teacher, instructing and helping design the systems, processes and technologies that bring a species peace, prosperity, long life and purpose through a connection with the Divine inside all of us. If you are a new human, you are one of these Souls.

Our numbers rose from thousands each year to now millions per year. The problem is many have never awakened to their true selves, and thus operate blind and frustrated in a world they do not understand and barely tolerate. They don't like Homo sapiens, but can't figure out why.

Many turn to drugs and alcohol to deaden the persistent feeling of unease and the pain of knowing there should be something more, but feeling helpless to do anything about it. That is where Kriya Serpent Yoga comes into play. Not only will it connect them to their Soul, and thus the Divine, but they will awaken to the reality of who they were, who they are and why they are here.

Once new humans remember past lives and see the Universal reality with clarity, they will embrace their purpose and begin the incremental changes that will end Homo sapiens. They will escape the illusions of this world, rejecting its ideals and impractical solutions to the problems Homo sapiens created. It is built into their DNA and is their destiny.

This transition may take a couple of hundred years, but will move us onto the next evolutionary stage of humanity. You will be a part of that transition and you will see the most amazing things you have never dreamed of. Homo illustratus will gain the wisdom to see beyond the veil that hides much of reality from us. They will join the Universe of other sentient beings and take a seat amongst those who govern this material plane.

If you think this all sounds like an episode of *Star Trek*, then I ask you where you think Gene Roddenberry came up with the ideas for that show? He was a new human, and knew a great many things others were not privy to.

There are roadblocks for the new humans, and Homo sapiens will not go quietly into the night. Using their dying breaths, they might very well try to destroy everything rather than give way to Homo illustratus. You know that ridiculous saying, "If I can't have it, no one can!" Imagine an ancient Homo sapien saying that with their finger on the proverbial button.

Good news, we do have Homo illustratus working within the existing political and military power structures, whether they know they are a new human or not, and ultimately, they will save us from the bombastic stupidity of the Homo sapiens in charge. I think you can name at least a few of those old Homo sapiens in charge.

Okay, so we awaken Homo illustratus, take over from Homo sapiens, and evolve into a future of technological innovation and Cosmic amity. So what makes Homo illustratus more capable to handle the complexity of this future world?

Good question. To understand it better, imagine a world where the following is commonplace:

- free and limitless energy;
- artificial intelligence not only sentient, but capable of thinking, analyzing, and processing at light speed;
- DNA modifications increasing humanity's physical, mental, and psychic attributes to adapt to myriad environments;

- DNA manipulation to cure most illnesses including old age;
- replication of food from raw, basic building blocks of biochemistry;
- billions of people who possess psychic abilities:
    - clairvoyance
    - remote viewing
    - empathic abilities
    - telepathic abilities
    - divination
    - channeling
    - telekinesis
    - astral projection
    - psychic healing
    - prophecy
    - manifesting
- antigravity;
- sonic alchemy;
- virtual reality indistinguishable from actual reality;
- inclusion into the Universal neighborhood with diverse life forms and cultures; and
- inter-galactic Travel.

These are Homo sapiens' worst nightmares come to life. Most of them can barely imagine such things, let alone manage and control them. Their ideas of control are suppression or elimination. Be certain of this, Homo illustratus will manage and control these things or earth will devolve into chaos, tribalism and war. It would cause a battle between those who have against those who have not.

We have all seen it play out in Hollywood films, which pit more advanced species against those who are less evolved. It never ends well on either side. But it doesn't have to be that way if we prepare humanity for these incredible revelations and creations.

That is where Homo illustratus comes into play. Not only can they easily imagine a world with such wonders in it, they are wondering why it hasn't happened yet. They understand the required ethics, morality and management of such incredible power, and will seek higher guidance.

New humans will build new structures of governance to ensure technology and abilities are used ethically with built-in safeguards to protect the Universe from consequences. Current politicians have all but ignored the Internet, resulting in chaos, division and death. But Homo illustratus will work with other species to gain their technology and acquire their wisdom to control it.

The Souls of Homo illustratus are ancient, and they have seen millions of incarnations and pitfalls from reaching the pinnacle of technological evolution. They see beyond the material plane into the ethereal, and know there is more than just the three-dimensional reality we currently believe.

Homo illustratus have worked with beings from different dimensions and timelines and do not fear them. They understand free will and how it changes the fabric of reality across all dimensions. The Universal energy flows through their material bodies, and they have already communed with the Universal consciousness to experience and understand unity.

Once they wake to their true self, all their memories and abilities will re-emerge so they can continue their work from previous lifetimes. They will build the framework of a new society and establish negotiations with other beings to help us enter the new age of humanity. This has all been prophesized, but most cannot read prophesies because of the illusion they are trapped within.

Yes, this is heavy stuff! But Homo illustratus were designed to make this happen successfully. They believe in humanity and its destiny, working tirelessly to manifest it. They have done this countless times throughout history, and we still see their fingerprints on megalithic sites around the world.

Homo sapiens cannot imagine, let alone work with all this. They still believe the lies about human history, ignoring the glaring evidence that stares them in the eyes, too afraid of what the truth will do if finally revealed. But revelations are coming, and they can no longer hide behind their fairy tales. This will change the world!

They will retreat to their caves, grab their guns, and wave their flags, firing on anyone who visits this planet without express permission. These people don't let fellow humans into their country, so God forbid an alien from another planet arrives.

Their time is over and they will have no choice but to step aside as Homo illustratus takes control of humanity's evolution. Sentient beings are already here, and they are watching to see who wins this evolutionary tug of war. They are not permitted to directly intervene, but they are watching.

Homo sapiens believe weapons will win the day, but they do not understand the people firing those weapons no longer believe in their lies and illusions, refusing to obey deadly orders. We already saw this in Russia when they invaded the Ukraine under Putin's narcissistic pretenses. The new humans in that country fled in terror lest they were forced to carry the stain of karma Putin's greed would inflict upon them.

In Iran, people revolted against the vile killing of a woman for not following their misogynistic dress code. These new humans see the tide of change and embrace it as the future they have been waiting for. They will no longer kill at the command of those whose greed powers this false and deadly world. Take away their armies, and you render them powerless. That is why Putin struggles and threatens nuclear war.

I know what you are thinking, but you are wrong. Homo illustratus will not go to war with Homo sapiens; it goes against their very nature and breaks all the natural laws they are here to protect and manifest. This takeover will be peaceful, though many will die as Homo sapiens lash out in anger and frustration as the end of their species bears down on them.

Mark these words, it will be the old guard who fires the first shots, killing their brothers and sisters in the name of humanity's survival. But they are really fighting for their own survival and power. Oligarchs, billionaires, narcissistic leaders, and petty dictators will all fall. Humanity will survive and thrive without the death and greed Homo sapiens inflict upon this world in the name of economic progress.

Will it be hard? Hell yes! Will it be worth it? Hell yes! Homo illustratus is just the being for the job. They are ready to use peaceful means, just like Mahatma Gandhi, to overthrow the tyrannical regimes around the globe and replace them with true democracy powered by those already connected with their Souls and the Divine.

I get it, there are wonderful Homo sapiens, and we will not deny them or belittle them as inferior, because they are not. They are simply unable to adapt to the rapidly changing landscape of our technology, culture and humanity. They are too slow, too stuck in their ways and unwilling to adapt.

Look around, they erect walls of resistance against everything changing in our world. They long for a lost age of innocence, yet another illusion to control and enslave. They dream of a mythical past when morality ruled, everything was perfect and there was order in their tiny world, controlled by their heavy hands.

That is a lost world of misogyny, racism, anger and war. They pine for conflict and violence because it is the only way they feel empowered. Control politics, control the economy, control religion, control morality, control behavior and control everyone. And when anyone steps out of line, crush them beneath your boots. Ah, the mythical lost paradise of Homo sapiens. *No thank you!*

I don't have to describe the inherent greed, lack of compassion and intolerance the old world contained. It is written in every history book and etched into the minds of all of us who lived through the last sixty-plus years. I wouldn't go back to any of those prior decades, for each contained their own follies and unenlightened cultural controls.

Some will call us agents of chaos, but nothing could be further from the truth. We are ancient agents of the Divine and follow the supreme plans of the Divine which does not tolerate chaos. Not only will we not support chaos, it is inherently impossible for Homo illustratus to do so. Oh, sure, we have free will, but we also have knowledge Homo sapiens do not possess and that alone is enough to ensure we would do nothing to put humanity in peril.

The question remains, can we stop Homo sapiens from destroying everything on their way out the door? We value life above everything and see it as Divine right. Homo illustratus could never destroy anything in return for their own enrichment, yet this is the very premise of Homo sapien society.

Once all of us are connected with the Divine, we act within the Spirit of the Divine and will not harm creation. That is why we will prevail and Homo sapiens will not. They know only destruction and greed and cannot fathom a world of peace and prosperity for all. They call it Socialism or Communism, trying to scare us with ancient tactics meant to divide so they can conquer. Don't fall for their traps.

We are backed by the true Creator of this Universe, and we have been contracted to uphold the very laws of that Universe to include the propagation of life and not the elimination of it.

Therefore, there will be no war with Homo illustratus. You do not need to fight to win when you are backed by that which created all things.

Yes, many Homo sapiens wave crosses and religious symbols to indicate they are backed by the Divine, but they act counter to the natural laws of the Universe established by the Divine they claim is backing them. They kill mercilessly (ISIS), and ignore the suffering of their brothers and sisters (billionaires), destroying anything that threatens their net worth and ancient structures (politicians).

Pure, human folly. Most of their religious constructs are politically motivated to suppress the individual and support the existing power structures. The Divine does not back their misdeeds and their illusions which hide reality from all they oppress. The great monoliths of their religious hubris will fall as Homo sapiens succumb to the sands of time.

For thousands of years, they kept secrets from all of humanity, demonizing anything that went against their dogma (inquisitions/witch-hunts). Even now, they make enemies of all who oppose them. Homo sapiens beat their chests like the great silverbacks of the Congo, threatening anyone who makes a move against their "harem." They jealously guard their riches and power, disregarding the Creator while lying to the world about their allegiance.

If need be, they will wave any flag to ensure their supremacy, and will tell any lie to ensure everyone beneath them falls into line or is crushed. I don't have to write down the names of all these people. We all know who they are, and we no longer want to follow them. We see through their illusions and houses of cards, and we know their end is near.

When the house of cards falls apart under the weight of their greed and avarice, it will be painful. Homo illustratus and many Homo sapiens will survive, but it will be Homo illustratus picking up the pieces because they were prepared and understand what is happening, why it is happening and what needs to be done afterwards.

The Divine is helping Homo sapiens' extinction through natural cataclysms that change the very face of our planet. The powerful and rich will hide themselves in caves built to sustain them through the disasters, but it will not save them. They will not inherit this world they tried to destroy.

They embody the things the Divine wishes to cleanse from this world, so they will be cleansed. Their own book, which they cling to as an insurance policy, outlines this in vivid detail, so they know it is coming. Remember, a rich man has as great a chance to ascend to heaven as a camel has to pass through the eye of a needle.

They don't want to believe in these prophesies, and most don't, but just in case, they wave the flag of religion around to convince the Divine to spare them from their folly. The Divine sees straight into your heart and through your delusional lies. If you truly cared, you would take care of this world and the brothers and sisters who live beside you. But you don't.

Look, the Divine does not want people to die, but when the evolutionary drain is clogged by a species that will destroy the world that protects them, then something must be done. Homo illustratus will be saved and a new book created which outlines how the new world should be rebuilt for the new humanity emerging from the ashes of the old.

Until that time arrives, Homo illustratus will be derided, demonized and terrorized by Homo sapiens. But do not worry, their efforts will never work. It cannot, for they are not the ones working for the Divine. Their power of manifesting is based on greed and selfishness and will no longer work in the coming age.

The more they grab control, the faster it will slip through their fingers. I believe many of them already realize their fate is at hand, which is why we hear such a fatalistic view within our world. Most people have received very little from these old Homo sapiens, and are beginning to realize the world they once believed in is all an illusion designed to control them.

It is a sad day when the con-man is found out, at least for the con-man. Everyone suffers, but at least they are free from the con.

The best part of this is you don't have to believe anything I say. But if you re-connect to the Divine through Kriya Serpent Yoga and awaken the new human within your DNA, this will all be revealed to you personally. Not from a human, but by the Spirit of the Divine Creator. Once it is revealed to you, you cannot and would not want to go back.

I love the metaphor of *The Matrix* movie trilogy for this very situation. As Morpheus said to Neo, "Remember, all I am offering you is the truth." And indeed, that is all I am offering you, the truth. Well new human, will you take the blue pill and return to your illusion of this false world or will you take the red pill and see how far this rabbit hole goes? The choice has always been yours to make.

Chapter 3

Dost thou love life? Then do not squander time,
for that's the stuff life is made of.
Benjamin Franklin

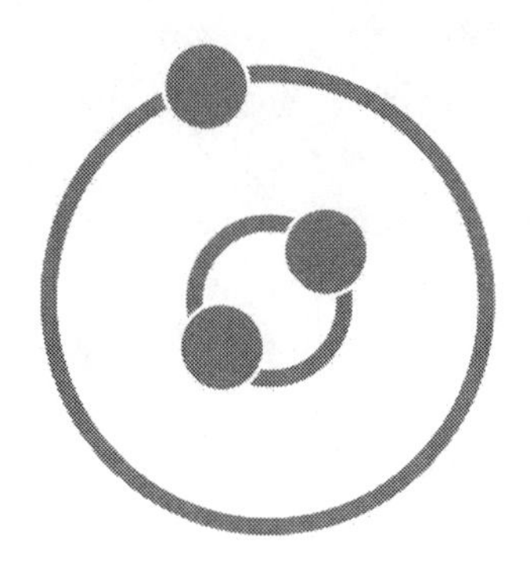

What Is Your Purpose?

Do you know your purpose in this lifetime? Most do not. We go through life in a blur of activities and events that are often quite mundane, unfulfilling and even depressing. Laundry comes to mind. Oh, sure, we have moments of happiness, but we don't have that ultimate feeling of happiness when we are engaged in our purpose. Once you have that, you will never "work" again. You know the saying, if you love what you do, you will never work a day in your life.

There are many people who know their purpose or stumble upon it somewhere during their lifetime. My father was a physician, and he was amazing. It was truly his calling, and he brought a lot of happiness to many people through his healing. He once delivered my friend's baby brother on Father's Day. He knew his purpose, and the Divine kept him alive longer than he should have lived to continue his work.

Gandhi, Mother Teresa, Jesus, Steve Jobs, Nikola Tesla, Albert Einstein, Madame Curie, Dr. Martin Luther King, Joan of Arc, George Washington, Gautama Buddha, are but a few of the millions who knew their purpose and pursued it until the end of their lives. My partner once exclaimed, "I cannot compare myself to these people." Anyone can be like them we simply have to answer the call.

But do we all have to change the world? The truth is, no matter how small or large our purpose, it is changing the world. Every new thought, invention, or way of looking at something old brings about small incremental changes to our world. Okay, if you live deep in the woods and never interact with the world, maybe you won't change the world, but that is probably because you weren't really pursuing your true purpose, anyway.

No act in the name of change is too small to have an impact. We talk about this in spiritual circles when we talk about intention and manifesting. It does not take everyone to shift the collective, only a small percentage of dedicated individuals. The schools of mysteries have known this for thousands of years and have flown under the radar, changing humanity little iotas at a time. Look at where it has brought us. Want to know who some of those mystics were. Here are but a few:

- Pythagoras,
- Paracelsus,
- Leonardo da Vinci,
- Isaac Newton,
- Dante Alighieri,
- Blaise Pascal,
- Napoleon Bonaparte,
- Rene Descartes,
- Francis Bacon,
- George Washington,
- Benjamin Franklin,

- Abraham Lincoln, and
- Walt Disney.

Well, you get the idea. These are people who believed in pushing humanity to greater heights. For the love of God, a couple of these people founded the United States of America! How is that for changing the world? Ever wonder why we have an Egyptian Obelisk as one of our US monuments? *The School of Mysteries!*

While I am a member of a school of mysteries to *re-learn* what I once knew in previous lifetimes, this is not a prerequisite for completing my purpose. You need not join a mystery school to achieve your purpose, but you might choose to join one later as you seek answers to everything you discover in your meditation practice. These discoveries change you in profound ways.

Let's be very clear about this. This meditation practice will change you physically, mentally and spiritually in ways you cannot yet fathom. While I cannot guarantee you will have the same experiences I have, you will have experiences. If you are one of the new humans who has manifested within the last thirty or forty years, then you are ready to be awakened and find your purpose.

To be honest, these new humans started manifesting as early as the 1800s, but their numbers were small, and the odds against them considerable. Much is still stacked against them today, but their numbers have grown, and they will soon be the norm rather than the exception.

Once the new humans reach a certain level, their intentions will tip the scales towards the new age of *Homo illustratus*. Homo sapiens will still exist, but they will fall in line as a new majority ushers them into a new future. This future is the new Age of Aquarius, an age when humanity finally ascends into the stars.

Your purpose plays a role in this process to help design and implement a new world. The changes are already starting as people realize you cannot pollute whenever and wherever you want. You cannot cause the extinction of existing species in the quest for your own selfish ends, and you cannot rule over everyone without them having a say in how they are governed. These old ways of Homo sapiens will end, and you will be at the forefront of this new evolution. Look around the globe and you already see the discontentment.

But first, we have to connect you to the Divine and your purpose. This book does just that. I will introduce you to the basic processes to help you find your purpose through both traditional and new meditation techniques imparted to me through visions. These are ancient methods that work and do not take a lifetime to master. They work so well and are so profound that I have them tattooed on my right forearm as a reminder of my quest to fulfill my purpose.

Now, it is not all easy breezy, though easier than you might think. Perhaps you hear only blah, blah, blah, and wonder where the meat is? Before we jump to the meat, I must warn you to move through the process slowly until you understand where you are in your spiritual evolution.

If you move too quickly, you may be scared off before you ever find your purpose, and we don't want that. Unpleasant side effects can manifest which may turn you away from the practice, and thus, your purpose. If you move too slow, you may turn away from the practice out of sheer boredom.

I get it. I can be a very impatient person, too. Just ask my wife if you ever run across her in one of your meditations. Continue reading, and I will walk you through the process and help you determine your practice and pacing. Keep in mind, it won't take decades, maybe not even years. Are you ready to peek behind the veil?

Chapter 4

Any man who reads too much and uses his own brain too little falls into lazy habits of thinking.
Albert Einstein

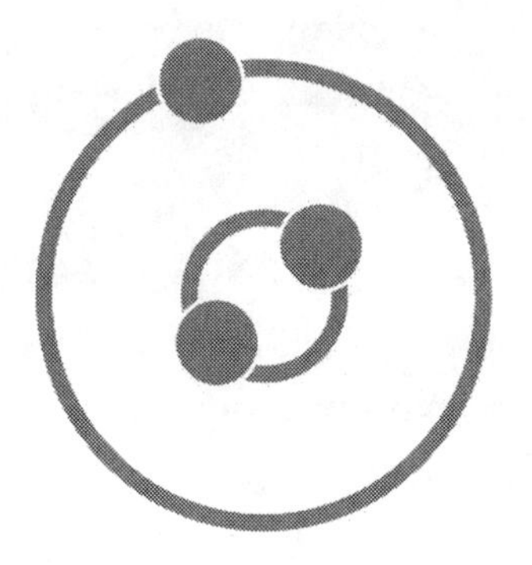

Where Do You Start?

I quote Albert Einstein because he is one of my favorite historical persons. Not because of his achievements, although they are great, but because he was as simple a human as they come. He embodied everything I am talking about and pursued his dreams while working as a patent clerk. He had a family, job, and all the trappings of life, but look at what he achieved. *Talk about passion!*

His quote warns us to avoid the pitfall of reading too many books, expecting enlightenment. Don't misunderstand me, I am an avid reader of many topics, and learning is a desirable trait. However, the proof is in the pudding! Book knowledge never trumps the experience of doing, and with Kriya Serpent Yoga, *you are doing*.

With that in mind, where do we begin this fantastical journey? Well, we begin with a simple test. Yes, doing is knowing, and knowing is critical to finding the starting point of your path.

The test is simple, and it will determine two things. First, are you Homo illustratus or Homo sapien? Second, how far along are you in your spiritual journey across many lifetimes?

If you are Homo sapien, your path will be longer and more difficult to travel. This doesn't mean abandon it, but reset your expectations while you enjoy the benefits of a steady yoga practice: better health and increased compassion for others. Aren't these worth pursuing?

Homos sapiens traveled down this path for thousands of years, being richly rewarded for their efforts. They evolved, eventually becoming the new humans of today. If you are one of these new humans, you will find your purpose quickly and reveal a Universe you could barely imagine.

This world is your inheritance, and you will soon join the fellowship of all peoples across the Cosmos. You will find your purpose and discover hidden talents you only glimpsed in your life. This is a Divine promise to all new humans who pursue the Divine within.

Kriya Serpent Yoga was designed for them, though other humans can benefit. Kriya Serpent Yoga is for advanced users who have achieved a lot in their spiritual evolution, much of that in past lives. In this incarnation, they are ready to attain advanced mastery of their etheric body, raising their overall vibrational energy to pierce all the planes of existence within the Universe.

I do not want to take anyone away from other practices and techniques. Indeed, though I received the knowledge of this gift, I still use other techniques learned earlier to enhance and support this new technique. Do not believe what you read here will be the end of all of this. This is an ever changing, evolving technique that ultimately will be extended as our knowledge and skills take us into higher planes of practice. But this is the place to start.

Okay, the following diagram is the test in all its glory:

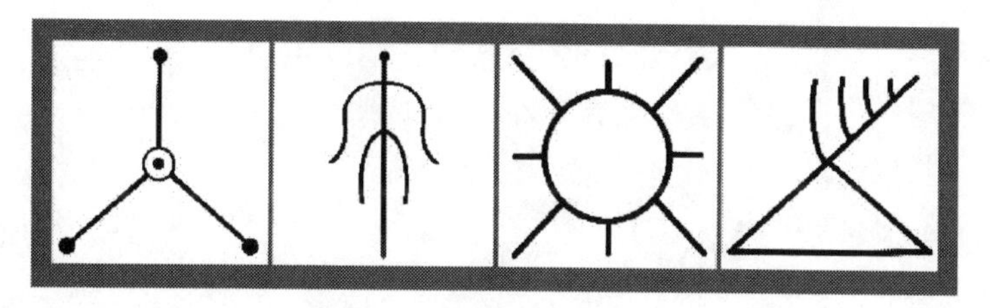

Can't read it? Neither could I. Before we begin the test, we must first familiarize ourselves with the symbols and sounds of Kriya Serpent. The four symbols above have a sound and a meaning associated with each of them. Though I won't reveal much about their history, I can tell you they are very ancient and have been missing from this world for a long time.

There was a time when Shamans used these symbols and sounds to connect with the Divine and seek guidance and meaning in their lives. That knowledge was lost a long time ago but is finally making a comeback at a time when humanity needs them. The sounds will be familiar as they are the basis of our vowels.

Now you might ask yourself if these sounds are made up to coincide with the fundamentals of human language or whether they are the foundations of early language development. I would posit that it is the latter based on how and where I received these symbols, their sounds and their meanings. Yes, even the symbols have power.

I feel that power in the symbols etched into my arm every time I meditate. The following contains the symbols, sounds and their meanings:

As you can see, very similar to A, E, I, O, U, except with sound and no I. Ohm you should already have heard of. It is the sound of the Universe, and is a staple in many meditations and chanting practices.

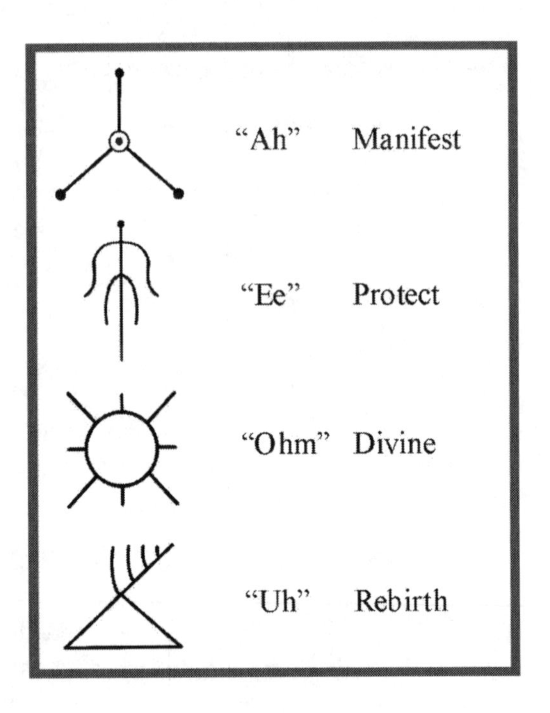

By the way, if you were wondering, I tested these on myself after I received them because I was skeptical even though they had been given to me in a very vivid meditative state. They work and like I said, I now have them permanently on my body.

This yoga practice is significant enough that I had it etched into my arm so that I could see it daily even outside of my practice. You may find that extreme, but that is how important it is to me. Once you test, you may discover the same thing. Okay, here it is. Complete it following all the steps exactly. Should take you around 5 minutes, but do not hurry.

The Test

1. Before you begin, establish a quiet place with a relaxed mood. After exercise is ideal, but as long as you have not been listening to loud and chaotic music, or just got home

from a vigorous day of work, you should be fine. Before bed is a great time to try this, as your body is preparing for sleep. However, if you are too sleepy, wait another day.

2. Sit comfortably with feet placed on the floor and back upright. You may sit cross-legged or in a half or full lotus position if you choose. You may also lie down. It doesn't matter, though most meditation techniques prefer sitting with straight back. If sitting, fold hands comfortably in your lap. If lying down, place hands on your belly but not overlapping.
3. Now close your eyes and slowly inhale deeply through the nose before exhaling through the mouth. Repeat this ten (10) times before moving to the next step.
4. Next, inhale deeply through the nose as before, but when you exhale, you will intone with your voice the sound of each symbol on the previous table. It will require four (4) exhalations to complete one (1) cycle of this (1 exhalation for each symbol). Complete ten (10) cycles:
    - breathe in and exhale, sounding **Ah**;
    - breathe in and exhale, **Ee**;
    - breathe in and exhale, **Ohm**; and
    - breathe in and exhale, **Uh**.
5. Intone the sound as long as you have breath before inhaling again. It should sound like a chant. Complete the sounds in each cycle in the order they are listed within the table.
6. Pay close attention to the sensations you experience while intoning the sounds. Identify what happens within each part of your body when you hear the sounds and feel the vibrations. Make a mental note of your experiences, including any visions, vibrations, sounds, muscle tensing, thermal sensations, altered states of consciousness, emotions or stirrings from within.

7. After ten (10) cycles, write or type the sensations you experienced while intoning the sounds for each symbol.

So, what are the sounds supposed to be doing? When intoned in the order listed above, the tones will begin to activate the life-force or *Kundalini* within you. This can manifest itself in myriad ways as listed below. Compare your notes of sensations with those within our list below:

- **sound**: buzzing, bells, wind, chimes, tinkling, water, tone;
- **touch**: tingling, numbness, tickle, electric, pressure, prickly, soft;
- **vision**: kaleidoscope, rainbows, shadows, faces, gray, black, white, flashes, swirling, falling, lifting;
- **state of consciousness**: clarity, sleep, meditative, calm, loving, charged, anxious, humorous;
- **vibrations**: pulsing, slow rhythm, tidal, static, electric, drumming, buzzing;
- **muscle tensing**: extremities, lower, middle, chest, neck, head;
- **thermal**: hot, cold, warm, cool, waves, dynamic;
- **stirrings**: inner movements or flow, creeping, liquid; and
- **emotions**: happy, sad, anger, fear, grief, love, compassion, empathy.

Understandably, some of these sensations are difficult to detect when you are not tuned into your senses. These sensations can also be caused by other stimuli which is why having a quiet and relaxed atmosphere is critical. Eliminating as many peripheral sensations makes the observations from this test easier and more accurate.

People already practicing meditation typically have an intimate knowledge of their base state, so they are more tuned in during the observations. If you're not, try your best and don't get discouraged. Remember, you may be a Homo sapien which may prevent you from experiencing any sensations at all.

Your location on your spiritual path has a direct impact on your experiences while doing the test. Those further along their path, even from previous incarnations, will probably experience greater sensations as they are tuned to the subtle energies within this exercise. It should be noted, this test is the foundation exercise in the basic Kriya Serpent Yoga. It is the beginning of the path to Kundalini. When combined with other traditional Kriya techniques you will activate and tune your etheric body.

Your experience will be different from others just as your appearance and voice are different. We incarnate into a new manifestation, and every manifestation differs from prior manifestations. After I received these symbols, sounds and meanings, I performed the test myself and experienced the following sensations:

- deep meditative state within 5 cycles;
- muscle tensing around Solar Plexus Chakra causing a tickle and desire to laugh (more on chakras later);
- my outer skin felt like it was electrified and numb;
- there was a pressure in my head and a feeling of love and compassion;
- my body was warm, but a cool wave flowed along my spine;
- there was movement in my Sacral Chakra as though something was stirring;
- I heard a constant hum; and
- a buzzing, static-like sensation ran throughout my body.

Keep in mind, when I experienced these sensations, I'd been meditating for nine years doing advanced bandhas in my Kriya Yoga practice. My expectations were higher based on my spiritual path. You may experience more or less based on your own journey.

While I had experienced Kundalini many times before the test, these other sensations didn't typically occur until 15–30 minutes within my practice. With the test, I experienced them within 5 minutes. That demonstrated the power of this technique compared to the traditional techniques I had been using.

After that initial test, I began the development of the *Song of the Serpent* and was blown away by the power I experienced during my first attempt. The Kundalini not only activated, but moved throughout my body readily, surging many times. Some surges were so powerful they took my breath away and tensed every muscle in my body. There is a reason I have it etched into my arm.

This test is not an exact diagnostic tool, but gives you a rough idea of where you are on your path to awakening the Kundalini, and gives you a suggested starting point to continue your journey, if you choose. And if you ask what journey, well, the one you have been on since you were created.

We can break down the sensations into the two main bodies of our being: *physical* and *etheric*. The *physical body* is the traditional five (5) senses we experience. The *etheric body* is the Soul or subtle body that senses metaphysical energies. Don't worry if you do not know or believe in such things, because if you are a new human, you soon will.

The following list breaks down the sensations between the two aspects of our bodies:

Physical Body

- sound,
- touch,
- vision,
- muscular, and
- thermal.

Etheric Body

- state of consciousness,
- emotions,
- vibrations,
- stirrings, and
- electric.

Based on the sensations of the two aspects of our being, we can determine where in Kriya Serpent Yoga you should begin your practice. As always, it is important that we are honest with ourselves and do not attempt more advanced techniques until we are ready.

This has been a common practice in the yogi-disciple paradigm of the past. The master would know when the disciple was ready to proceed further. Don't worry, you will know when you are ready. Based on the experiences during your test, the following gives you a general guideline of where you should start if you wish to do this practice:

1. Level 1: **Introductory**
    - 0 etheric sensations, or
    - 0–2 physical sensations.
2. Level 2: **Beginner**
    - 1–2 etheric sensations, or
    - 1–3 physical sensations.
3. Level 3: **Intermediate**
    - 3 or more etheric sensations, or
    - 4 or more physical sensations.
4. Level 4: **Advanced**
    - full Kundalini activation.

Again, do not stress about your starting point. Depending on the current path of your spiritual journey, you may find moving up through the various levels happens in as little as a few months, but not longer than a few years. Is that not worth it for the benefits of finding your purpose and connecting to the Divine? I think it is a small price to pay for so much to gain, but you will have to be the judge.

If you are truly one of the new humans, you will probably fall into the Intermediate to Advanced level. If you fall into the Introductory level but are young, don't worry, we can help you start your journey. More than likely, you will quickly advance through all the levels.

What once took decades for the old humans will now take only a few years for the new humans. Their DNA is more evolved, and therefore so are their physical and etheric bodies. They will attune themselves to the Cosmic energy faster with greater efficiency than older humans.

If you are not a new human, it may be better starting with more traditional methods rather than Kriya Serpent Yoga. When the two aspects of your being are not ready for Kundalini, it is dangerous to activate it. It may lead to physical, mental and psychic harm which will inhibit your journey. Start on a more traditional path as preparation. There was a reason yoga masters of the past were measured with their instructions.

After consulting the list above, you should have determined a starting point for your spiritual journey. Each level provides a simple process to follow. Remember, your goal is to awaken your Kundalini, connect to the Divine and find your purpose in this incarnation. Once that happens, you will experience the most amazing things. You will feel such love, bliss, and clarity of spirit and mind that you will wonder how you ever lived before that point. I sincerely hope you start this journey.

One last word—even if your starting point is intermediate or advanced, it is best to read the preceding levels to familiarize yourself with the overall practice. I urge you to read all the levels' techniques and mastery so you can test yourself before starting on a higher level. I offer instruction on some of the basic Kriya Yoga techniques I integrated into my practice, and they may serve you in your practice. I am not suggesting you have to start at Introductory, but it is worth the read.

Chapter 5

The wave is the same as the ocean, though it is not the whole ocean. So each wave of creation is a part of the eternal Ocean of Spirit. The Ocean can exist without the waves, but the waves cannot exist without the Ocean.

Paramahansa Yogananda

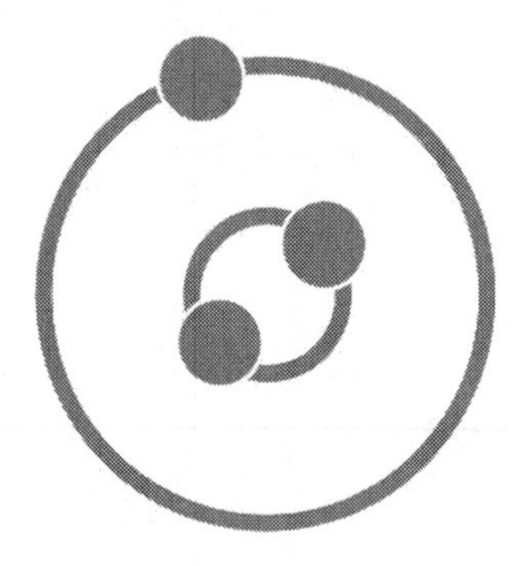

The Science of Kriya Yoga

Before we begin, we need some grounding in the science around transcendental meditation. Much of it revolves around the Pineal Gland, something everyone possesses. This gland is part of the endocrine system and regulates our brain chemistry, such as serotonin and melatonin. It is the gland which regulates our sleep cycle, releasing melatonin each night to cause drowsiness. This is part of the famous Circadian Rhythm.

Afraid you're reliving your human anatomy class? I promise to keep it brief. However, I need to highlight some aspects of the Pineal Gland that directly affect the mind during meditation. The stimulation of this gland is critical to activating Kundalini, and there are various techniques which cause this stimulation.

Let's first look at the structure of the Pineal Gland and point out some of the interesting parts of this tiny region of our brain. First, it is called pineal because it is shaped like a pine cone. It lies behind the Thalamus at the top of the brainstem and is covered with tiny, hair-like follicles.

The Egyptian Eye of Horus has a remarkable resemblance to a cross section of this region in the brain and shows the exceptional knowledge ancient Egyptians possessed in describing the central nervous system. Many mystical scholars and yogis have talked about it as the seat of the Soul, but I think of it as a connector to the Soul.

Stimulation of the Pineal Gland causes the creation of melatonin, an important chemical regulating sleep and activating our body's healing regeneration. A side effect of Kriya Yoga is excellent sleep, so deep and regenerative, you'll need fewer hours to feel rested.

The changes in cerebrospinal fluids which produce experiences of higher levels of consciousness are attributed to the Pineal Gland. It is these higher states where Kriya Yoga plays an active role. Various meditations and bandhas move the cerebrospinal fluids up the spinal column into the Pineal Gland, stimulating hormone production to produce these relaxing states of higher consciousness.

These higher states of consciousness are necessary to re-connect us with the Divine to learn the guidance It has for us. I say re-connected because there was a time when this was a common daily practice among people led by the shamans of old. Unfortunately, much of it was lost throughout time because of ignorance and dogmatic preaching.

Thankfully, many of the yogis in the East kept the knowledge alive and only taught it to those who were far along their spiritual path. That was then. This is now. With Homo illustratus, the gurus are inside, and one need only achieve transcendental states to connect with the Divine.

Kriya Yoga is one of those practices that can help you achieve that, but Kriya Serpent Yoga is an ancient technique that will help new humans achieve results that once took lifetimes to achieve. At the time of this writing, I am likely the only human on earth that knows of this technique, let alone practices it. I hope this book changes that, and that you will soon enjoy the benefits of this yoga technique.

This yoga is ready to re-integrate into society once again. There is nothing like the Divine connection and clarity achieved through this practice. I am addicted to Kundalini, but what I really mean is I am addicted to the constant presence of the Divine within. It provides you with clear purpose, something I've never experienced prior to practicing this yoga. You will enjoy these benefits, especially once your true purpose is revealed.

Yoga Primer

So, let's start this journey with a primer. That is to say, let's talk a little about the nuts and bolts of yoga. Yoga is a set of disciplines designed to create a healthy human who is happy and connected with the Divine aspects inside all humans. Much of yoga stemmed from many practices dedicated to Hinduism and later branched out, as many Buddhists practiced much of the same disciplines based upon the teachings of Buddha. These practices have spread, evolved and are practiced in nearly all parts of the world.

I believe Hinduism is important knowledge steeped in mythologies of deities, where Brahman was the ultimate deity. These lesser deities often taught knowledge and technologies that, to primitive humans, seemed like magic. However, that knowledge, including yoga, made humans healthier and ultimately happier. The gods provided a user manual for the human body and spirit.

In Buddhism, Siddhartha Gautama became disillusioned with his life, despite an abundance of earthly pleasures. Leaving that life behind, he sought meaning within the religious practices of his day. He wanted to understand the ultimate truth of reality and his existence.

But his search was disappointing, until one day he achieved his enlightenment while meditating under a Bodhi tree. That enlightenment led to his philosophical teachings which were a departure from a deity based belief to one of self-enlightenment. He realized humans were the creators of their own reality, destiny and happiness.

This was a fundamental shift from the philosophies of that time, placing reality under our control. It taught us the ego, our self in the material plane, controlled all our life experiences. Understanding the ego allowed you to control your existence. This was a direct departure from a deity based philosophy where nothing was within your control, and the only way to enhance your reality was through appeasing the gods.

With this evolutionary shift, yoga evolved. Many began to call it the *science of yoga,* since it was a scientific method to improve physical and psychological health. It taught people how to be the best version of themselves, controlling their own health and happiness without the need of a deity. This was significant, and Buddhism is a significant practice in our modern world, gaining new practitioners every single day.

When I started down the Buddhist path before Kriya Yoga, I discovered a form of enlightenment simply by shifting my paradigm. Buddhism is still a significant part of my practice, because no matter how much I have learned about reality, Divinity, and the Universe, I am still learning how to control my ego. We all are.

Today, another shift is taking place, and this began when yogis from the East brought their philosophies and practices to the West. They taught everyone there was a part of the Divine within them. It gives us life and is the only eternal part of us. In modern religions, they call the Divine part of us the Soul.

This is a fundamental teaching of Gnostic Christians who were once hunted down by the Catholic Church for their "blasphemous" ideology. It is not blasphemous, but a reality the church suppressed for thousands of years. Mystics and those who follow the true teachings of Jesus understand this. These philosophies were handed down through the mystery schools since the dynastic period in ancient Egypt.

These yogis believed the Soul is a fractional part of the Divine whole, or to put it in words you might understand, your Soul is a small piece of God. You are an expression of the Divine. Therefore, if you connect directly to your Soul, you connect with the Divine. Yes, you can speak to God through your Soul, a part of God within you.

Now, if you are an atheist, why are you here? Intellectual curiosity? By now, you are probably ready to hang it up. If so, peace be with you. However, if you are truly curious, continue onward. I find most atheists shutdown as soon as you mention a Divine Intelligence. They believe it is ancient, mythological voodoo, but I believe the Divine is an Architect or Engineer of this incredible creation we call our Universe.

Time to put all the cards on the table. An intelligence designed the Universe to define itself through experiential means. It created myriad pieces of itself that attempt to define themselves by experiential means. It would be like splitting yourself into a hundred pieces, sending each one on a different vacation. When they all returned, you would remember everything they had done, expanding your understanding and experiential evolution in the process.

I imagine you are thinking, "I cannot split myself!", so the idea is ludicrous. Or is it? Imagine each incarnation is a piece of a whole. Then each incarnation is an expression of you wherein you experience something different every time you incarnate. When that life is over, those experiences integrate back into your whole, which we call the Soul. That is why your spiritual journey is over many lifetimes.

So, the Divine expresses itself through myriad pieces of its whole (Souls), through complex lifeforms expressing themselves through myriad pieces of their Souls (incarnations). If you dig deeper, there is a larger reality beyond our Universe which expresses itself through myriad pieces of itself (Creators). For all we know, this goes up and down infinitely like a fractal, but we need not concern ourselves with that philosophy, for it does not offer us benefit other than intellectual and philosophical curiosity.

Okay, either your mind is blown, or you are ready to run for the hills. Bear with me, it will all make sense once you connect with your Soul (Divine). Your material self is composed of an ego, or mind that is part of the material plane. It is the five senses we know and love: *sight, sound, touch, smell* and *taste*.

When we are born into this body, our ego is the mind created through a lifetime of experiences. We all love the ego, because we love all the experiences we gain from it. At least I do. But the ego is also the cause of the suffering in our lives.

The Soul is an esoteric energy with vibrations and consciousness. It resides within the ethereal plane rather than the material plane. This ethereal plane is real, and consciousness is a fundamental aspect of that. *We think, therefore we are!* Understanding consciousness is critical to understanding the Universe. Nothing exists without consciousness.

It is the glue that holds everything together. In the physical plane, we now know everything is almost nothing. Remember? Energy and emptiness? Consciousness created the Universe, and it is the building blocks of reality. Physicists are just beginning to scratch the surface of how consciousness affects matter, but it does affect matter. A new science will soon emerge from this reality.

Perhaps you see where all this is going. We want to attain higher levels of consciousness to rise above the material world of the ego, so that we can realize our true Divine nature (Soul), and help others achieve the same thing. That is our spiritual journey of experiences. Our self-expression through many lifetimes. That provides self-expression for our Creator, therefore, our Creator helps us along this journey.

Hinduism, Buddhism, Taoism, Christianity, Islam, Judaism or any religion you wish to tout are expressions of this fundamental truth. Each presents a different path to get where you want to go, some faster and with a bit more help from the Creator. I believe Kriya Serpent Yoga is the fastest method to connect you with the Divine so you can seek guidance and knowledge to create your own reality.

I am not here to convince you of these truths. You already have your own beliefs formed by your ego over your lifetime. But if you are not satisfied, then don't stop looking, keep forging ahead, learning more and experiencing more, and you will end up in the same place, maybe a different lifetime from now.

Now, most religious leaders or yogis do not just throw all of this in your lap on day one, but my *purpose* in this incarnation is to wake up the sleeping new humans, connect them with the Divine part of themselves so they learn their purpose, and then provide them with the tools they need to accomplish that purpose, whatever it might be.

I am not here to indoctrinate you into some hybrid religion. In fact, I am not here to offer you religion at all. I am here to tell you that the Divine is real, and you can connect to It and learn these truths for yourself. Just like Buddhism, you are the one that controls this, not me and not the Divine. *Nobody but you!*

Yes, I have seen the future of humanity and know where we are headed and what we become. Sure, I can tell you about other beings which exist in the material and ethereal planes, and what their role in humanity's evolution is. Yes, I can tell you about all the magic that exists because of consciousness, and that you can do this magic using your own consciousness.

I can tell you many things about reality, but ultimately it means nothing until you experience it for yourself, and that is all I am offering, a chance to experience it for yourself. Yoga contains the tools to enable you to experience true reality through a direct connection with the Divine. If not in this lifetime, then in a future lifetime because we are all a part of that Divine, and we are driven to experience life before returning to the unity of Source. At our choosing, we embark on another adventure (incarnation), continuing our evolution.

I promise you, once you start down the spiritual path of yoga, you will emerge an enlightened human. Even Homo sapien will one day become Homo illustratus, but some simply take a little longer than others. This practice will make you happier, healthier and a better version of yourself. In the end, you will truly love life like no one who has yet to start their spiritual journey.

Try Kriya Serpent Yoga. If you dislike the changes it makes within you, stop and go your own way, seeking your own path. Free will is a Universal Law, and you can exercise it anytime you want. You want to be enlightened, choose to be enlightened. You want to be ignorant, then be ignorant and let your ego lead you wherever it chooses, experiencing all the material world offers. Because no matter what path you take, that path will be experiential, and ultimately, that is why we are all here.

Now that I have put it all on your shoulders, you decide. Should you continue reading? Your mission is to try our techniques, connect with your Soul and find your purpose. From there, you will decide how, where and when you fulfill that purpose.

We will be here to help, because we are all connecting to the same Divine. Therefore, all our purposes are aligned to the betterment of humanity. Whether or not that means we work together depends on what your purpose is and what it requires.

As I have said before, I am not recruiting worshippers, religious zealots, or any followers other than those who have spoken with the Divine and follow their true purpose. I want only what is best for humanity, and right now, we aren't cutting it, and the new humans know that. We can do better. We will do better, and Kriya Serpent Yoga is how we make that happen. Buckle in. The adventure is about to begin.

However, without a brief introduction to the energy centers of the body, which we call the *chakras*, we cannot fully discuss Kriya Serpent Yoga. Since the purpose of our yoga is to stimulate the life-force or Kundalini, we must understand the chakras through which this energy flows. The next section presents an overview of these energy centers and how Kriya Serpent Yoga activates them.

Chakras

Thousands of years ago, humans mapped the subtle energies of the body, documenting them in the ancient Hindu Vedas. Some believe the chakras are energy centers of the body which control and direct subtle energies, regulating our bodily processes such as our hormonal and neural systems.

While there are over a hundred different chakras, most yoga practitioners focus on the *seven* major chakras listed below from bottom to top of the body:

1. Muladhara,
2. Svadhisthana,
3. Manipura,
4. Anahata,
5. Vishuddha,

6. Ajna, and
7. Sahasrara.

Struggling with the names? So did I. Fortunately, we have anglicized these names. I should note that the study of chakras and their relationship to health and healing in the body is quite vast, and for some, it is their purpose to study and practice techniques to accomplish healthy chakras and thus, a healthy body.

I will not intrude on these practitioners nor steal their thunder. Their work, as others with purpose, is to further our knowledge of these energy systems so we can enhance our life and spiritual existence. If you are interested in this topic, refer to the resource section at the back of the book for additional material on the subject.

In Kriya Serpent Yoga, we are concerned with the location of these major energy centers. Three of them in particular are the main focus of our practice. Below, I list the English names given to these main chakras and a brief description of their location, color and relationship to your physical and psychological health.

1. **Root (Muladhara)**: Red color located at base of spine near tailbone. It is associated with your physical identity, stability and grounding.
2. **Sacral (Svadhistana)**: Orange color located below the belly button just above the pubic area. It is associated with pleasure, sexuality and creativity.
3. **Solar Plexus (Manipura)**: Yellow color located in the upper abdomen near stomach. It is associated with self-esteem and confidence.
4. **Heart (Anahata)**: Green color located center of chest above heart. It is associated with love, empathy and compassion.
5. **Throat (Vishuddha)**: Blue color located at the throat. It is associated with communication.
6. **Third Eye (Ajna)**: Indigo color located in the center of the brain behind the eyes. It is associated with intuition and imagination.
7. **Crown (Sahasrara)**: Violet or white color located at the top of the head. It is associated with awareness and intelligence.

Keeping them balanced is a key aspect of these energy centers. Kriya Serpent Yoga is concerned with several of these chakras in particular: Heart, Third Eye and Crown. The other chakras are important, and our techniques activate them when we channel energy up and down the spinal column.

For Kundalini, we focus on the three chakras listed above based on their associated relationships to our spiritual and psychological states. Kriya Yoga is similar in this respect. The heart and brain regions are critical to our spiritual evolution, and we activate them through our practice to gain benefit and to access the Kundalini.

Our energy work aligns the energy system, benefitting all your major chakras, eventually affecting all chakras within your body. Though we do not focus on all chakras, your work with the subtle energies tunes all of them, yielding overall health benefits. Many gurus in the past were often associated with wonderful health, including some who lived long beyond ordinary lifespans.

At the risk of sounding like a broken record, we are not concerned with the health benefits of this practice, but rather the connection with the Divine and our life's purpose. We view these side benefits as simply that, benefits, not the main purpose behind the practice.

However, do your own research if interested. Kriya Serpent Yoga never prohibits the use of other yogic techniques. In most instances, these other techniques may benefit your Kriya Serpent practice as well. After all, a sound mind and body are foundational to success in your spiritual pursuits.

Since I have mentioned Kundalini many times, it is imperative I give you a cursory introduction to this life-force energy so critical to the stated goals in Kriya Serpent Yoga.

Kundalini

Kundalini is often represented by a coiled serpent at the Base or Sacral chakra. When it rises like a cobra ready to strike, it sends essential energy through our main chakras. Because our yoga is associated with Kundalini, I have called it *Kriya Serpent Yoga*.

I named it *Kriya* because of its association with Kriya Yoga and *Serpent* because of its relationship to Kundalini. While traditional Kriya Yoga stimulates the Kundalini for similar reasons, Kriya Serpent Yoga is a more expedient technique to achieve identical results. This means fewer techniques and less time to achieve results.

People may scoff at this attempt to speed up the process by casting aside a traditional yogi-disciple modality, and I completely understand their wrath at what may be viewed as blasphemy. But I contend there is a clear imperative why this new yoga is necessary.

Kundalini is within all of us and accessing it is a fundamental right of our Divine nature. As humanity's evolution undergoes this current transition, speed is necessary to usher in the new as the old passes into history. One need not devote themselves to a guru in an ashram to find their purpose in this lifetime.

A lifetime of dedicated practice to find your purpose is both impractical and unsustainable. Our world rushes headlong into an exponential growth of technological innovations. We enjoy (some say suffer) this technological renaissance but it requires an enlightened populace to adapt quickly. If we cannot, we will fall victim to this technology rather than benefitting from it.

Imagine the world of artificial intelligence (sentience), mind controlling matter, interstellar travel and extraterrestrial relationships. Homo sapiens are not up to the task, especially when they operate at speed magnitudes slower than our current technological progress.

This will bury us if we do not achieve a level of enlightenment quickly. We must use our inner connection with the Divine to handle this new reality with wisdom and finesse to ensure our species' survival.

I am not a doom and gloom kind of guy, but we are light years behind our technology, which is already demonstrating its ability to destroy our society because of our ignorance. This is another part of my purpose but beyond the scope of this book. However, if you are interested, check out www.InstituteForHumanEvolution.org to learn more.

Back to Kundalini. It is best described as the life-force. Yes, kind of like the force in Star Wars, but geared to enlightenment rather than lifting rocks. It is the creative force of life, and you have experienced it as a part of an orgasm. Its power is undeniable, and its association with the orgasm has often been its demise.

Though you can easily access it through sexual techniques, those techniques aren't our methodology or purpose. Like the health benefits mentioned earlier, sexual benefits are simply a side benefit. Unfortunately, that relationship with sexuality has been used to denigrate Kundalini and its practitioners even though we use it for Divine outcomes.

Like all things in life, corruption and abuse of power has tainted Kundalini in the eyes of many. Homo sapiens still have a very immature relationship with sexuality because of dogmatic teachings that have told us it is wrong and evil. That is nonsense.

But again, not our purpose for using Kundalini. This powerful life-force, endowed within us by our Creator, is used to help attune our subtle body to the energies of the Universe, thus removing the veil that hides the truth from us. It should not surprise anyone that you need a great deal of energy to access higher states of consciousness and thus higher planes of existence. Kundalini is that energy.

By using pranayama, we pass the Kundalini through our chakras to achieve higher states of consciousness. This affords us access to higher planes of existence where we learn the truths about our reality, the Universe and our purpose within it. We can tap into the Universal consciousness to gain wisdom.

All sounds great, doesn't it? But before we run off and start pumping energy through our chakras, we must be prepared for it. Just as a high-powered lineman must prepare for the extreme voltages and currents flowing through the lines, we must take precautions to ensure we do not "shock" our system with Kundalini. While death is not necessarily a concern, there can be physical and psychological damage if we are not properly prepared.

Though ethereal, Kundalini is real energy with real consequences. Chakras are energy centers with direct interactions to various physical parts of your body, so damaging these energy centers could manifest damage to those physical parts. Our greatest concern is the nervous system and brain. Since the nervous system connects all your body's hardware to the brain, great care is required before we engage those systems.

This is why yogis were measured in their introduction and preparation of the disciple before activating Kundalini. But now you are your own guru, so exercise similar precautions. As both yogi and disciple, you must be measured in your introduction to Kundalini. You do not want to hurt yourself, just as you wouldn't want to hurt anyone else.

All practitioners should be physically mature. Everyone should be at least eighteen years old and far enough removed from puberty to have some degree of focus. Ideally, a person would be in their early twenties before practicing Kriya Serpent Yoga, but some new humans could start at eighteen.

If you are under eighteen, prepare first through traditional yoga and Buddhist techniques. Learn them while you are young and apply them when you're older and physically capable of handling the rigors of Kundalini. There is much to learn, and Kundalini will be a graduation present from that earlier work.

Where you are on your spiritual path has a direct correlation to your readiness for Kundalini. Too close to the beginning of your path, and you are not yet ready for all that energy. Further along, and you can handle the energy as you once did in previous incarnations. As I stated before, new humans are further along than Homo sapiens, therefore, most will be ready right out of the gate.

However, the new humans have dealt with a world that does not fit them, and that has often caused all sorts of distress. This distress manifests psychological maladies, which can make one less prepared for Kundalini. I suffered extreme anxiety for years, and it was severe enough to require prescription medications.

However, I found the cure was worse than the disease and quickly learned to manage my anxiety with my mind. This was a necessary transformation for me to prepare for Kriya Yoga and Kundalini. However, anxiety is a potential problem for the new humans incarnating into our world today.

This will become less of a concern as we expand our education of young humans to prepare for the connection to the Divine through Kundalini. If you are a new human who suffers anxiety, you need to start at *Introductory Level 1* to ensure you are ready for Kundalini. It may take you longer, but the results will speak for themselves.

I must emphasize, psychological and physical readiness is critical. Just as an abused instrument will not sound its best, your own instrument (body and mind) must be in good condition for it to perform properly. You don't have to be an athlete, but you should improve your physical condition while working on your spiritual evolution. This is discussed later within the sections of the Kriya Serpent techniques.

However, psychological health is imperative. Though practicing Kriya Serpent Yoga will improve your psychological well-being, if you come into it with poor health, your existing conditions could be aggravated rather than improved. That might throw you off the practice, thus inhibiting your spiritual progress.

Discuss this with your health professional if you have even the slightest concern. Being committed to a mental health facility because of your initial efforts will delay your journey along the path or stop it altogether. That would be counter to your goals, so exercise common sense and be overly cautious before starting this practice.

I made sure my health issues were sufficiently taken care of before I traveled down this path and I didn't know the risks at the outset. Now that I do, I am relating those concerns to you based on my own experiences.

Let's dig into a few of the effects of Kundalini on the mind and body, so you are more informed.

Anxiety, Depression and Mania

Increased energy surging through your system may trigger the *flight or fight* response, and this triggered anxiety feels scary if you are not prepared. Be aware that it is temporary and will pass, but it can be intense. I find exercise or calming music a great way to ease this anxiety, but those sometimes further stimulate the Kundalini, so take care of how much and what type.

Bipolar depression, which I suffer from, manifests as episodic mania and depression. I found Kundalini often pushed each end of that spectrum further out, *increasing* the effects of my illness. I quickly learned consistent treatment was essential in managing these extremes while continuing my practice.

The good news is these effects are temporary, so you know they will subside. I use a broad spectrum CBD to treat my condition with amazing results, but this may not be for everyone. Ask your doctor about appropriate treatment or consult an herbalist for alternative natural remedies for your particular conditions.

Because preexisting conditions may be aggravated rather than resolved by Kundalini, you should be well versed in your illness and have effective treatments to manage it successfully without powerful side effects.

When in doubt, take periodic breaks from your daily practice if your condition worsens. These side effects will subside and you can return to the practice afterwards. Over time, this will cease to be a problem as your body adjusts to the increased energy.

Repressed Trauma, Grief, Karma and Painful Memories

This is a natural part of the Kundalini process, but it can be disturbing if you are not prepared beforehand. It is an essential part of the healing process and our continued evolution through dealing with our traumas and karma. Reliving those painful experiences and shame is part of that process. We must accept this and know that over time the Kundalini will burn them from our being through this natural energy "fire."

In the Buddhist practice of Nicheren Daishonin, karma manifests as difficult life conditions which you deal with to fully process the karma. With Kundalini, however, you relive it but do not manifest poor life conditions. The Kundalini burns your karma away, freeing you to pursue your purpose rather than dealing with negative life conditions. It is an easier and better way to deal with past karma, especially for those far along their spiritual path.

Don't misunderstand me, the other methods strengthen you to be more resilient, but if you are a new human, you achieved all this in prior incarnations. Now, you are ready to focus on your true purpose in this incarnation. Despite that, you must still deal with traumas from this current incarnation, and reliving that trauma can be painful.

Traumas are those things that have been done to us, those things we have done to ourselves, and things we have done to others. Early in my practice, these traumas surfaced, and I spent a lot of time resolving them before I could move forward. If needed, consult a therapist who can help you work through these traumas. You must be able to deal with them if you are to grow into who you really are.

Grief was especially difficult for me. Even ten years after my wife passed away, I still suffered grief in a way that affected my life and my relationships. It all resurfaced in a big way as I began my Kundalini practice, but I was fortunate to meet someone who was also struggling with grief, and helping them helped me. Today, I have nothing but fond memories of my time with my wife and I am no longer disabled by her death.

Physical Pain and Health

It is important you understand preexisting conditions may be aggravated rather than relieved by Kundalini. If your body is not ready for Kundalini (poor circulatory or nervous system), then your conditions may get worse.

I recommend achieving good physical health before beginning this practice. Physical yoga or other forms of exercise are excellent ways to strengthen your body and heal preexisting conditions. Always consult a physician before beginning a new exercise regimen, and start slowly. Over time, you will benefit from your efforts and build the needed attributes for handling Kundalini.

However, you do not need to delay your Kundalini practice until you are healthy, but you should focus on the basic aspects of meditation instead of Kundalini. These basic skills prepare your mind for the journey into transcendental states of consciousness. Breathing, focus and stillness skills are essential to prepare you, and these can be completed while getting your health into a stable condition.

Remember, Kriya Serpent Yoga takes less time than traditional techniques, but may still take years to fully benefit. Patience and preparation are critical to this speedier success. Remember, measuring your spiritual growth in years is far better than decades. If you are a new human, your body will know when you are physically ready for Kundalini.

Trust the process and enjoy the full journey rather than the final destination. Over time, Kundalini will transform you both physically and psychologically, causing a more positive, healthy life state from this practice. But if you rush the process, you may delay it further.

Whether we want to agree with it or not, diet is an important part of health. Are you a vegetarian? Vegan? Pescatarian? Maybe an omnivore? I am an omnivore but was raised in a religion predominantly vegetarian. My maternal grandparents were vegetarians their whole life, and I still have family members who are vegetarians. I have eaten plenty of wonderful vegetarian meals and aspire to be vegetarian. Let's call my shift to vegetarianism a work in progress.

I am not a dietician and do not speak with authority on this subject other than my own life experiences and basic science, which I call common sense. What you put into your body impacts your health, and the lower the nutrients, the lower your state of life will be.

If you put poisonous materials into your body, then they will degrade your autonomic systems, causing a lower life expectancy and life state. There is a common sense saying in engineering parlance, "Garbage in, garbage out." Just because it is deemed safe by our regulating authorities does not mean it is safe for long-term consumption. The problem is the cumulative effects over time.

Eat an overly processed salted snack loaded with fat, and you will live to tell the tale. Eat it everyday for twenty to forty years, and you may not live to tell that tale. You see, most regulatory bodies are not concerned with the long-term cumulative effects as much as is it safe to eat now?

They are putting the responsibility in your hands as to how much and how often you eat such things. Don't get me wrong, I love a good chip now and then, but I don't eat them daily.

So what does this mean? It means *you are responsible* for your life state and condition. You can't just eat anything you like and then complain about a poor life state, blaming it on your genetics, your living conditions, or some conspiracy within the food industry.

You need to accept the fact that much of the processed consumer foods produced today are filled with garbage you don't want in your body. Take responsibility for how much you consume of these foods to save yourself from the garbage. Free will is a Universal Law, but you must use your Divine given intelligence to exercise it wisely.

Here is my take on food. Only eat natural foods not processed and loaded with additional substances such as preservatives, coloring, artificial flavors and sweeteners. The USA, my home country, has been battling an epidemic of obesity and cancer for decades due to these overly processed foods which people gobble up without a thought. Blame the companies all you want, but ultimately, it is your hands putting that poison into your mouth.

Many people experience poor life states because of their overindulgence of these foods that mostly contain carbohydrates, a substance our bodies naturally store as energy reserves (fat). Because of this overindulgence, obesity has caused a spike in Type II Diabetes and heart disease. It is literally killing people. I love doughnuts, but not enough to die from them.

Now I ask you plainly, how well do you believe your body will handle the ethereal energy of Kundalini when it is struggling to survive from such a poor life state? *Not well.* Eat fresh foods, not food loaded with things you would never eat if they were placed in a bottle and put in front of you. Yet, when they hide in our processed foods, we gobble them up like mana from heaven. They are not from heaven.

Food portions are just as critical in our pursuit of health, and I am as guilty as the next person. Yes, we all have our idiosyncratic methods for dealing with stress, trauma and self-esteem issues, but eating our emotions does not lift us to higher life states. Therefore, we cannot connect with the Divine and pursue our life's purpose. Eating smaller portions and snacking less often helps us achieve a balanced life state, supporting our spiritual efforts.

And that is what this book is all about: our *spiritual evolution*. Does that mean you can't enjoy a soda now and again? No. Does it mean you have to live off of rice cakes that taste like sawdust? No. You can enjoy what you want, but you must take responsibility and control of how much, what kind and how often.

If eating is a problem, and your current life state requires you to deal with obesity, seek professional help in dealing with that as you start your spiritual journey. Poor health will lower your overall life state and energy, significantly slowing your spiritual progress. Paramahansa Yogananda said in his autobiography that you need not give up all your worldly pleasures to pursue your spiritual path, but the further down the path you travel, the less you will crave those worldly pleasures.

After I put on 25 extra pounds during the Covid-19 pandemic, I sought tools to help me take that weight off. One thing I found that worked for me was intermittent fasting. Search it online. For me, I do not eat for 16 consecutive hours each day. I have mostly given up snacks (only occasionally), and try to control my portions. As a teacher, this can be a struggle when boxes of doughnuts seem to appear in the teachers' lounge regularly.

Since practicing Kriya Serpent Yoga, I have noticed both physical and psychological changes within me. Cravings of any kind (food or otherwise) have diminished by more than half. I no longer enjoy cigars, and they make me very ill if I do smoke one. My body no longer tolerates the poisons inherent in tobacco. I gave up drinking completely, and on the very rare occasions I have a drink with friends, the effects are not pleasant, especially the day after.

As you tune your body to the ethereal energy of Kundalini or any energy within the Universe, you achieve a higher life state within the material body. It changes you in such a way that you crave healthy choices rather than unhealthy choices. It is not even a conscious choice but a reaction to the physical changes taking place within you. Your body wants a higher state of life, and you can achieve it through yoga.

Before I end this, I must address eating animals and animal byproducts. As we evolve as a species, it is natural for higher beings to want to protect and defend all life, not just their own kind. In this vein, you can see why eating other animals or enslaving them for the production of food would be considered less evolved. And I agree with this wholeheartedly but have yet to put my evolved sensibilities into actual practice.

I don't want anyone who professes they are a new human to look down upon anyone who still eats animals and animal byproducts. As mentioned earlier, we are all on a different path in our journey, and some are more evolved than others when it comes to diet. As the collective changes, so will those, like myself, who are stuck in our indoctrinated ways. Show us the way peacefully, and we will eventually all follow you as we evolve through our practice.

The changes are happening, so the process is moving, but it will be a long time before we clear this hurdle. Science and technology will lead us to the finish line once we learn to manipulate matter to create whatever we wish without the need of living beings. Think *Star Trek* replicators and you get my gist.

More than anything, peace must be a cornerstone of our practice. We must not reprimand those who are further back on their path, or those who outright oppose us. Evolutionary change can be a slow process, but it will happen whether people want it or not. How do I know? Because we will evolve into higher beings within the Cosmos, we will become more enlightened about everything, especially food. I admire those who are Vegan, but I am not there yet.

Kriya Serpent Equipment

As far as equipment is concerned, Kriya Serpent Yoga does not differ from other meditation techniques. There is a basic list of items to acquire, though some may be replaced with common household items. However, in the long term, you will want dedicated equipment which you can easily acquire for reasonable cost online.

The following is a list of items you need for your Kriya Serpent Yoga practice:

1. **Zabuton**: Meditation cushion you can acquire for around $25–$100 USD.
2. **Zafu**: Round meditation seat cushion placed on top of a zabuton. Cost can range from $25–$100 USD.
3. **Wool Blanket**: Prevents grounding of energy. It can range between $25–$300 USD depending on what type, quality, and pattern you are shopping for.
4. **Mala Beads**: These are used to count repetitions in our techniques and can be found for around $35–$200 depending on the style and bead composition.
5. **Ear Plugs**: Though optional, I recommend them for your practice. You can buy them online for around $5–$40 USD.

A few comments about this equipment. First, some prefer meditation on a chair instead of a meditation cushion. People with limited mobility and/or flexibility usually require a chair. Since this is a practice for all, use a chair if you must. However, make the chair straight-backed with a comfortable seat cushion and a height so your feet rest flat on the floor. The chair may either have arms or not, but you will probably find it easier to use without arms.

Myself, I used both a zabuton and a zafu, but both wore out and no longer served me. As I have aged, my flexibility in the legs has been impacted, but I have not moved into a chair.

Instead, I simply purchased a 4-inch thick piece of memory foam and cut it into an appropriate shape for my sacred space. I covered it in the wool blanket and placed a different zafu on top. Works perfect.

The wool blanket for preventing your energy from grounding is critical. In fact, I suspect my early efforts in Kriya Yoga did not yield advanced results due to me not using the recommended wool blanket. Once I integrated a wool blanket into my practice, the energy went off the charts.

If using a chair, drape the wool blanket over the seat cushion, letting it hang over the front of the chair to form a place to put your feet on it on the floor. For a zabuton, simply cover the entire seating area with the wool blanket.

Mala counting beads are essential for keeping track of your repetitions throughout your practice. A standard set of Mala beads contains 108 beads plus a guru bead (starting point) attached to strings with ending beads and/or a tassel. They come in various materials such as wood, crystals and stone. I use Sandalwood mala beads which are smooth and have a wonderful scent. Get some you like, but you don't really need to be extravagant unless that is your style.

I have read a lot about ear plugs used during meditation but I will present my take and let you decide for yourself. A lot of meditation techniques do not support earplugs since recognizing the environmental noise around you and learning to train your brain to ignore it has beneficial effects. However, in Kriya Serpent Yoga, we are primarily interested in achieving Kundalini as quickly as possible so we can connect with the Divine and find our purpose.

With that in mind, earplugs could be considered a cheat or hack to achieve that goal. They are beneficial for me to disconnect from the external stimuli while I meditate. I have children, pets and noisy neighbors which easily delay reaching deeper states of consciousness. Yes, I could learn to filter them out, but that would be more challenging and take longer. I am a parent and teacher, so my ears are constantly on high alert.

Earplugs are sold in bulk and cost little, so try them and see which you prefer, with or without. It does not make a significant difference in your Kriya Serpent Yoga practice, but if you are going for a higher state of spiritual vibration, training to meditate without them is probably the way to go. It will not affect Kundalini either way, but may take you a bit longer.

The following are *optional items* I recommend, but you decide which you want to use. I believe in long-term benefit from these additions, but early on, they are unnecessary:

1. **Altar**: Small table for holding your spiritual equipment such as incense, beads, etc. You can get one for around $50–$1000 USD depending on size and composition. Some have elaborate carvings on them, thus raising the price significantly.
2. **Incense**: Smell is a unique sense to engage while meditating. I recommend Sandalwood, but many prefer Patchouli. They can be bought for around $5–$20 USD.
3. **Incense Holder**: Holds the incense and collects the ashes. You can find them for $10–$40 USD depending on the style, size and composition. Mine is a small bowl with a Sanskrit letter painted on it.
4. **Crystals**: Not everyone believes in crystal energy, but I am devout. I recommend amethyst and quartz. These can range from $10–$300 USD depending on quality and size.
5. **Reading Light**: If you share a sacred space with someone else and meditate early in the morning or late at night, get a small light for your altar so you don't disturb your partner. These can easily be found for around $10–$20 USD.

Long term, an altar is a fantastic addition to your spiritual practice. Mine pulls double duty as my sanctum for my mystical practice. I keep all my spiritual paraphernalia on my altar, and it is a focal point for my practice. I found an inexpensive Asian coffee table that works great for my altar. You can go simple or fantastically extravagant with carved exotic wood. It doesn't matter so long as it serves your needs, matches your overall décor and makes you happy.

There is a lot to be learned about crystals, and I have only scratched the surface. The way they emit, channel, cleanse, and focus energy is quite amazing. As you advance in your Kriya Serpent practice, you will notice you can detect and discern these crystal energies which may have no effect on you right now. After my initial Kundalini experiences, I was blown away when I walked into a crystal shop. The energy within the shop was a physical force that overwhelmed me. I had to step out and take a break while my daughters shopped.

I am able to handle that intense energy now. Seek advice when buying crystals, as some contain toxins and require special care you need to be aware of. I use amethyst to help elevate my state of consciousness by amplifying energy. I use clear quartz crystals to cleanse negative energy from my spiritual objects, other crystals and my chakras (in Advanced Level of Kriya Serpent Yoga). You don't need them starting out, but later they benefit your practice.

If you are really just starting, begin simple and spend as little as possible. It does you no good to overspend on something that only requires yourself, a blanket and a chair. However, these tools I recommend will not go wasted and provide benefit in your practice long term. You can refer to the *Resources* chapter at the end of the book for a few places where you can shop for these items, but simple searches online yield plenty of results.

Chapter 6

If you can't fly, then run. If you can't run, then walk. If you can't walk, then crawl, but by all means, keep moving.

Dr. Martin King Jr.

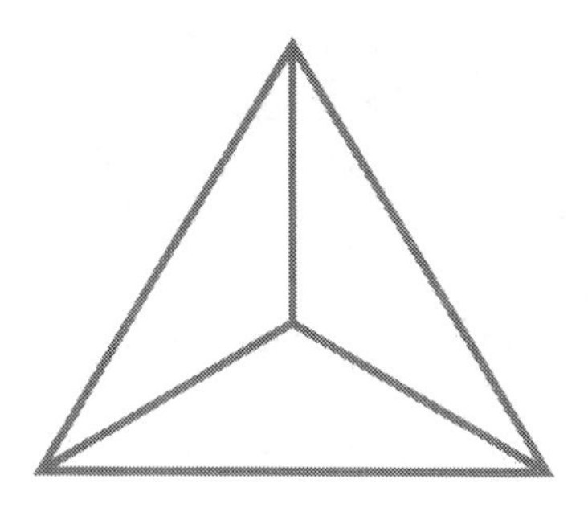

Introductory Level 1

Introduction

As the quote of this chapter would imply, keep moving. By that, I mean keep evolving spiritually. This level is the very starting point of a spiritual path. You may find yourself here at this point in time, but that does not preclude you from achieving higher levels sooner than you might think. Again, it has to do with where you are on your path across many lifetimes, not just the here and now.

I spent much of my life completely oblivious that a path even existed. I was asleep and hadn't yet awakened to my prior lives and the path they had set me on. Once this was revealed to me, I was off to the races. You may fall under the same category, asleep, but once awakened, watch out!

Unfortunately, it could be the opposite, and this is your very first incarnation where you start your spiritual path. Revel in that fact and don't look at it as some sort of failure on your part. If you never start, you will never awaken in this life or future ones.

I know this sounds like so much of the dogma inherent in many religions, suffer now and you will find paradise later, but that is not how it works, nor how you should view it. Look at it as the very beginning, and learn where it can go. If not in this lifetime, then many lifetimes in the future. You will benefit in the here and now—you need not suffer.

One of the most fundamental aspects of Buddhism is the premise that suffering is caused by ourselves, rather than by external things. It is how we react to the external world that causes our suffering. With Kriya Serpent Yoga, how you react will shift dramatically, and from that shift, you will find happiness emerging within your life. Real, unadulterated happiness. If that is not worth it, I guess I don't know what is.

There are additional benefits other than happiness. You might activate your siddhis, or latent abilities within all humans. Today, we know these as psychic abilities which are currently the subject of scientific study under the name Noetic Sciences. They are real, and when you experience them, it will open up the Universe and reality for you. What you think reality is, isn't the true reality. Once you connect to the Divine, you will learn more.

I would be remiss if I did not mention the more mundane yet amazing benefits of this practice. You will be a more relaxed and stress-free human. Talk to anyone who practices yoga, they are often the most chilled people around. And I want to stress this point. Yoga is both a set of fitness regimens and meditation techniques. But Kriya Serpent Yoga is a specific yoga practice that focuses only on *transcendental meditation.*

The fitness of traditional yoga is excellent, and I have practiced that off and on for many decades—long before I ever meditated. This book does not discuss yoga fitness since there are ample resources for you to access. Other benefits include the aforementioned sleep, but it goes deeper than just great sleep and regeneration. Lucid dreaming and vivid dreams are likely.

Lucid dreaming is waking while in the dream state, and there is nothing like it. I suggest you search online for more information about that incredible subject.

Some benefits are more esoteric, and may not mean much to you now, but once you find your purpose, they become important. These are increased compassion and empathy towards all beings, but especially humans. Yes, you will find love for your fellow humans and eventually extend that to all living beings.

That compassion will manifest a true happiness within you. This is not a temporary happiness like riding a rollercoaster or making love but a permanent, significant happiness. If you find your purpose and pursue it, you will have lasting happiness the rest of your life—guaranteed.

These are benefits that all people experience at some point when traveling this spiritual path. For some, they don't care so much about spirituality, compassion, or anything esoteric. For one, it may go against some of their long-held beliefs. I get it, and this book is not for them. If they are not ready to travel down this spiritual path, that is okay.

But you? You took the time to read up to this point, so you must have some interest in esoteric things. In fact, maybe you have experienced some of the same things I have, and you are questioning your own beliefs and understandings of reality. If that is true, then you have come to the right place. Don't worry if you are not a new human, you will still benefit in this lifetime.

Alright, let's do it! For consistency, I have broken each level into several sections:

- Introduction,
- Objective Skills,
- Traditional Techniques,
- Kriya Serpent Techniques,

- Suggested Daily Regimen,
- Warnings, Suggestions and Side Effects, and
- Expectations for the next level.

Please read through all sections in each level before starting the actual practice. It will give you an overall introduction to the practice and present recommended daily regimens to make the most of your efforts. This will inform you of the potential side effects which may manifest and how to address them.

Objective Skills

If you are just starting your spiritual journey, then you have various skills which must be developed before starting Kriya Serpent Yoga. Not that you can't learn the Kriya Serpent techniques, but you will not benefit from them since you have not fully prepared for Kundalini.

If you are reading this as I recommended and have already done meditation and/or tested into higher levels of Kriya Serpent, then you should move on to the next technique. However, if you have not mastered the skills in this level, then spend time at this level mastering them. These techniques are not all Kriya Serpent specific, and many originate from other disciplines. Mastering them will help you achieve the prerequisites for Kriya Serpent Yoga.

It is assumed you have a good working knowledge of each of the objective skills, if not mastery, before moving to higher levels. If you have not mastered or used these techniques before, please do so before proceeding. It is important you have prepared yourself before you move to the higher levels. Let's look at the main objective skills you need to achieve before you move onward into those higher levels of Kriya Serpent Yoga:

1. **Sit in meditation**: Basic sitting technique for all meditation practices. *Mastery* is achieved when you can sit comfortably

without moving or discomfort for the entirety of your session.

2. **Counting beads**: Counting is important for all techniques. *Mastery* is counting the repetitions of all techniques using beads with eyes closed.
3. **Quiet monkey mind**: The human mind is a thought generator, and silencing the monkey chatter permits us to meditate. *Mastery* is attained when you can sustain 15 minutes with very little to no thoughts.
4. **Focus**: Focus and visualization go hand in hand as requisite skills to enter transcendental states. Mastery is visualizing a detailed object and its properties for 10 minutes.
5. **Identify chakras**: Identify main chakras and locate them within your body. This is critical to stimulating Kundalini. *Mastery* is the ability to easily place your focus on each chakra and sense it.
6. **Breath control**: Breathing is an integral part of meditation. *Mastery* is when you can easily perform each breathing technique.
7. **Basic Kriya Serpent**: Learn the symbols, sounds and meanings of Kriya Serpent Yoga. *Mastery* is when you can intone all the sounds while visualizing the associated symbols.

The first thing most beginners want to know is how long learning and mastering each technique takes. That is subjective, and in the past, a master would have differing times for differing devotees. The same applies here, so the best I can give you is a general guideline of 6–18 months.

Homo sapiens will probably take 18 months to master these skills while Homo illustratus will take less time. As I mentioned earlier, learning the fundamentals is key to success, so don't be discouraged. Practice regularly and earnestly, and you will make steady progress.

The following details each of the objective skills and the techniques you should use to achieve that skill. The actual techniques are outlined later in the *Techniques* sections.

Counting Beads

Keeping count of repetitions is an important part of any meditation practice, but especially Kriya Serpent Yoga which has specific numbers of repetitions. Once you have Mala Beads, practice the technique to familiarize yourself with counting while meditating. It should be automatic in higher levels of practice, so practicing early helps develop the automatic repetition.

After this level, you should be capable of counting up and down for various counts accurately without looking. This is a fundamental skill in most Buddhist practices.

The Monkey Mind

Whether or not we want to admit it, we are descended from apes and have much of the same instinctual habits they do. A constantly chattering mind is one such thing. It is a survival skill to be constantly vigilant for danger and planning your next meal. Without those thoughts directing you, your survival may not be guaranteed.

The human mind is much the same, but most of us have evolved beyond the ordinary concerns of monkeys. Instead, our minds are preoccupied with the day-to-day minutiae and stresses of our modern societies. Work, education, family, friends, home, chores, health, diet and vanity are all major drivers in our lives. These preoccupy our minds with thoughts that cannot be silenced even when we try to relax or sleep.

This is a problem in meditation, as it keeps our minds from focusing on deeper states of consciousness. Think about the millions who suffer from sleep deprivation because of overly active monkey minds. Even now, I lose sleep when difficulties at work overwhelm me. It is a real problem, and we must all learn to control the monkey mind if we are serious about traveling the spiritual path.

Now, add to the monkey chatter the entrainment that occurs when we are consumed by our technology. The unchecked use of such devices creates entrainment within the mind to think little and shift focus often. While they may be impressive skills for quickly streaming through mindless content or gaming, they are debilitating to your overall brain function. If you suffer from this addiction, you need to reduce your use of such technology or you may never achieve proper meditation.

Think of entrainment as creating grooves (connections) in your brain like grooves in the musical records of old. Depending on the grooves, you get different outputs. Entrainment is how your brain learns. However, if you learn to only focus your attention for a few seconds at a time, then you are entraining your brain into the worst kind of monkey mind, one that chatters at speeds beyond reason.

This is why research shows an enormous increase in ADD (Attention Deficit Disorder), ADHD (Attention Deficit Hyperactive Disorder), anxiety and depression from the heavy use of technology, especially the consumption of social media. Do yourself a favor, cut your use of these things in half. Once you begin your spiritual evolution, you will lose interest in these bobbles that do not engage your mind in positive ways.

Gaming is no different, and I know this from experience. After years of intense gaming, everything I did in my life began to feel like a game. While gaming strategies can be important in our lives, it is ultimately a very narrow view of how we should think and live.

To quiet the monkey mind is probably the hardest technique to master for most humans. As a single parent, full-time teacher, technologist and writer, my mind has always been racing at the speed of light. I thought it was cool being able to out-think those around me with this speedy mind, but it brought on more problems than it could solve. I have since slowed my thinking significantly and apply a lot more conscious thought with better results.

When I first started Zen meditation, I found it nearly impossible to quiet my monkey mind. My mind was like a cell phone with notifications enabled. I couldn't shut them off or turn the volume down. It limited my focus and made my meditation neither relaxing nor rejuvenating. Instead, it was more like work.

You will probably find the same thing, and it will be the hardest skill at this level to achieve. It nearly forced me to give up meditation, but I persisted and eventually mastered it. However, it took longer than I expected.

Don't get frustrated. You can learn this, and once you do, it will change you in very positive and significant ways. It will reduce your anxiety, make you far more patient with others, and cause you to be more thoughtful about how you deal with other people and situations. The following techniques will help you master this skill.

1. **Focused Breathing**: You will complete 5–10 minutes of this technique which originates from Zen Buddhism.
2. **Emptiness**: You will learn to clear the mind and maintain a state of emptiness (or near emptiness) for 10–15 minutes. This also originates from Zen Buddhism.

Focus

Focus is fundamental for life and proves invaluable on your spiritual journey. Imagine Astral Projection without focus. Who knows where you might end up, assuming you're able to perform Astral Projection at all?

Some people have amazing focus, but many do not. It is especially missing in many within the younger generations. As a secondary school teacher for over twenty years, I have seen the curse of the inattentive disorders. The students' ability to get anything done, learn anything new, or take part in group activities is seriously compromised by their condition.

While there are techniques these students can learn to help them overcome this disability, it is still quite difficult and often results in students never fully achieving the heights their intellect affords them. Throw an addictive distraction like modern technology on top of this condition, and you have a recipe for disaster. Just ask a parent with a student who suffers from ADD.

The key to focus within Kriya Serpent Yoga is to set the mind to a singular task or state. It makes us more receptive to entering different states of consciousness to contact our Soul. As mentioned before, when you move on to more advanced mystical studies, focus is fundamental to achieving most of the results.

If you can, reduce your use of distracting technologies and learn to focus your mind. Remember, when you use such technology excessively, you are literally training your brain to *not focus* as you zip through content at lightning speeds.

I realize many believe this technology is life, but it is nothing more than an illusion of life. In fact, when you stare at a screen darting from one thing to the next in a matter of seconds, you are purposely turning off your mind and not living at all. You become a zombie.

Ever see people at restaurants staring at their devices while ignoring everyone around them? That is not living. Why go out with people if you have no intention of interacting with them? Stay at home and be the lone zombie you were meant to be. Relive that pandemic experience.

Focus helps you in your spiritual practice, your educational pursuits and your professional life. No one is looking for workers who can't pay attention in meetings, forget what they are supposed to do, or wander off while in the middle of a conversation. It may work when around other zombies, but for the rest of us, it is incredibly hard to take you seriously.

Inattention is a childish attribute and one you must learn to outgrow if you wish to evolve into the being you can become. No one will go to their grave looking back on a life solely devoted to staring at a device and a stream of mindless images and videos thinking that was a good life. That is not a life but self-delusion. Put your device away and live in the real world. It is quite wonderful.

The following techniques will help you with focus.

1. **Visualization**: You will learn to sustain 10–15 minutes visualizing detailed objects within your mind. This stems from various techniques used in modern psychology.
2. **Sensing the Present**: You will learn to spend 10–15 minutes being present and paying attention to the world around you. This originates from esoteric practices through mystery schools.

Chakra Identification

Kriya Serpent Yoga uses our main chakras to stimulate Kundalini. Because of this, it is critical to have a working knowledge of each chakra and its location before attempting advanced techniques. It may appear overwhelming at first glance, but it is rather easy to achieve this skill with consistent practice and focus.

Since we are dealing with vibrational energies, we can think of the chakras as the sweet spot for a specific note on a stringed instrument. Miss the exact spot, and you get a sound that is close but not quite right. Hit the sweet spot perfectly, and beautiful music emanates from the instrument. Chakras are like that. Finding them is like learning where the sweet spots are on an instrument. Let the vibrations lead you. The following technique will help you identify your main chakras:

1. **Om Japa**: You will sustain 10–15 minutes of this technique which originally comes from Kriya Yoga.

Breath Control

Breathing is absolutely fundamental to meditation. There are different breathing techniques you can learn that will help you with other techniques of meditation. At this level, we will touch only on simple techniques to start. In subsequent levels, we will introduce additional techniques to boost your efforts.

As you breathe, you oxygenate your blood and bring that oxygen to all the cells in your body. By that very simple fact, you are nourishing your cells and improving your life state through breath. Yes, it is necessary for life, but more than that, breathing can help open up your etheric energy pathways, calm your monkey mind and improve focus. These are essential for Kriya Serpent Yoga.

Your body has been changed throughout your life by lifestyle choices and environments that often shut down your etheric energy pathways. These blocks prevent you from fully benefitting from the energy and cause chronic conditions that don't seem to have known underlying causes. In Kriya Serpent, as in Kriya Yoga, we want your pathways and chakras to be healthy, not blocked, so they pass the etheric energy easily through the body to improve your life state and practice.

Breathing brings necessary oxygen to the areas of the body where your energies flow. Healthy cells in those areas assist the energy flow as they achieve higher levels of vibration from their improved life state. It is like replacing old clogged pipes with new ones to improve the flow of water. While breathing is only one aspect of this, it is an essential part of your overall health.

In meditation, calming the mind by controlling your breathing assists you in achieving the states of consciousness desired. Think about it, how many times have you heard someone say stop, take a breath and calm down. Breathing is an essential tool for controlling your emotional, physical and mental states of consciousness.

If you read about sleep cycles, you'll note that breathing is integral to the different states of consciousness we achieve while sleeping. That is why people who suffer from sleep apnea do not achieve healthy sleep. They are interrupting their natural sleep cycles through the interruption of their breathing. In yoga as in sleep, breathing is important.

The following techniques will assist you with your breathing during your meditation.

1. **Deep Breathing**: You will learn to perform 12 counts of this technique borrowed from Zen Buddhism.
2. **Nadi Shodhana**: You will complete 12 counts of this technique regularly. This technique comes from Kriya Yoga.

Basic Kriya Serpent

This technique is akin to the test you took earlier. This is a very basic skill and will help you later when you no longer intone the sounds verbally, but mentally. Sound is vibration and vibration is critical to practice. We can eventually entrain that sound within our minds and still benefit from the vibrations without the need to vocalize. This is your initial step into this practice. This technique is outlined later in the Kriya Serpent section.

Traditional Techniques

Sitting in Meditation

Sitting in meditation can be done either on a zabuton or on a chair. I do not recommend using a bed or lying down on anything. Sitting with back straight should be your goal. Understandably, some may find it difficult to sit with a straight back without support. If that is you, then use a chair and slide back so the backrest supports you fully. Obviously, use a chair with a relatively straight backrest or place something like a pillow between you and the backrest for support.

1. When sitting in meditation, wear loose-fitting clothes. Anything which binds or restricts blood flow makes it impossible to achieve relaxed states which are necessary in meditation.
2. Sit on a zabuton or chair covered by a wool blanket. If sitting on zabuton, cross legs as you normally would, or sit in a half or full lotus position. Lotus positions are unnecessary in Kriya Serpent Yoga. Over time, any of these sitting positions will become easier for you as your body stretches. On a chair, sit with feet flat on the floor on top of the wool blanket.
3. Hold Mala Beads in both hands with a curled forefinger on bottom and thumb on top, resting in the gap between the guru bead and the first bead on the left and right.
4. Straighten back (don't slump), and tilt head down slightly as though staring at a distant object on the floor.
5. Close your eyes and relax all tension from your body while maintaining a straight back. *Stare inwardly up at the point of your forehead between your eyes.* This point is called **Bhrumadhya** and is the **focal point** during your meditation.

6. If you feel any discomfort, adjust your seating before practice. If you cannot eliminate the discomfort, you may need a different sitting position or place to sit.

Switch to a chair if you cannot sit on a zabuton in a cross-legged position. You can always switch back to the zabuton after stretching exercises to help you achieve the floor positions. The key word here is comfort. Without that, you will probably have a difficult time focusing or relaxing in meditation as your body screams in pain.

At the start of your practice, assess your current energy state. Note the energy feelings within you. Are they low, high, anxious, sleepy? What about your emotions? You want to establish a baseline of your spiritual energy and emotions so you can properly observe them after your practice. This provides feedback on your spiritual progress. Over time, you will feel increased energy and emotional stability after each practice.

Once you have completed your meditation session and before you get up from your seated position, assess your energy and emotions again. What is different? How do they make you feel? What are you thinking about? Monitoring these changes in each session can not only help you monitor your spiritual progress, but can be a huge motivator to continue your practice when life is trying to stop it. While I can tell you what you may experience, it is you who must truly experience it.

Counting Up and Down

The following exercise helps you learn to use bead counting to keep track of repetitions while meditating. You want this to be automatic when you meditate, because if it is not, you will constantly fiddle with the beads and count instead of focusing on the meditation techniques.

1. Sit in meditation.
2. Using either your left or right hand, use the opposite hand to slide the beads through your thumb and forefinger counting each gap you go through. Stop when you count up to the desired number.
3. Place the opposite hand in position between your start bead and the next bead after it.
4. Using the fingers you counted up with, inhale normally and then exhale, clawing back one bead at a time, counting verbally or mentally until you get back to the guru bead where you started the count. Obviously, the count should end with the same number you started with.

The following are the levels you should achieve with this technique. Start slowly and work your way up:

- **Beginner**: 12 counts,
- **Intermediate**: 24 counts, and
- **Advanced**: 48 counts.

With practice, counting down becomes easier as your fingers learn to claw back each bead. Over time, it becomes automatic, and your mind will not think about it or the count. Start at beginner and integrate into your daily practice, increasing the count as it becomes more automatic. If your count down does not match your count up, it isn't the end of the world, but attempt to make them match.

All counts are multiples of twelve. The exception is Nadi Shodhana Pranayama, where a starting count of six is acceptable in daily meditation.

Focused Breathing

The following are the steps to focused breathing. It is a simple technique with various benefits:

1. Sit in meditation.
2. Count up beads.
3. Inhale deeply through your nose while focusing on the tip of your nose and the sensations you feel there. Hold breath for two counts before proceeding.
4. Exhale through mouth while focusing on the breath as it is released. Hold after exhalation for two counts while counting down your beads by one.
5. Repeat steps 3–4 until total count down is complete.

The following are the levels you should achieve with this technique. Start slowly and work your way up:

- **Beginner**: 12 counts,
- **Intermediate**: 24 counts, and
- **Advanced**: 36 counts.

As you focus on your nose during inhalations and exhalations, you will quiet the mind. Over time, you will see a subsequent decrease in the chatter. Move up through the counts as you achieve a marked *decrease* in the chatter for the current count. This technique is excellent for quieting the monkey mind and increasing focus.

Emptiness

To fully quiet the monkey mind, you will attempt to achieve a state of emptiness. That is a mind with no thoughts. For me, the best method is visualizing a black void in my mind's eye.

1. Sit in meditation.
2. Visualize a black void in your mind's eye.
3. As thoughts slide into view, imagine them sliding back out, replaced by the black void. Ignore the thought, don't get frustrated because it appeared, or rush it away in

anger. Quiet all emotions surrounding the thought, for it is an *independent* object rather than something of yours.

The following are the levels you should achieve with this technique. Start slowly and work your way up:

- **Beginner**: 12 counts,
- **Intermediate**: 24 counts, and
- **Advanced**: 36 counts.

As you practice this earnestly, you will see a significant slowdown in the thoughts that appear. Keep the focus on the black void you created and keeping it black by removing thoughts. Eventually, you find that stillness where only you exist and your thoughts have dissipated. It will take time, but so worth it to the future of your meditation practice. Be patient.

Some may view the black void as something negative, but nothing could be further from the truth. We are trying to eliminate sensory stimuli, thus darkness or black is the absence of light stimulating our eyes. When you first close your eyes, you see colors and shades of brightness based on a residual image within your optic sensors. We want to eliminate that residual image and all other sources of stimulation, thus black is the absence of that. It is not negative, just the removal of everything.

It is a wondrous moment in your practice when the monkey chatter really subsides. You feel a release of stress, a connection to your inner self and the beginnings of establishing a connection with your Soul. It is baby steps, but the beginning of something beautiful.

Visualization

Visualization is a fundamental aspect of meditation and most mystical practices. It is used throughout guided meditations and often included in therapeutic techniques intended to alter negative thinking into positive thoughts. You will use visualization to increase your focus, which you need in more advanced practices.

1. Sit in meditation.
2. Create the black void in your mind's eye.
3. Picture a small seedling tree constantly growing into a large tree that eventually towers over you in the blackness.
4. Once the tree is fully grown, look down at the roots sinking into the blackness below you. Focus on the texture of the bark, its color, the shape of the root and its size. Circle the tree looking at each root in the same way until you have fully analyzed each one, and the picture of those roots in your mind's eye has crystalized into something tangible and clear.
5. Lift your eyes and look at the enormous trunk of the tree. Notice the texture of its bark, the color, any knots or inconsistencies. Estimate how wide the trunk is and then follow it up slowly until you reach the first branches. How far up have you looked? Has the trunk crystalized into something tangible in your mind's eye?
6. Look at the branches. Count how many there are. Pick one branch and follow it up and out, choosing another branch when it splits, making a path up into the canopy. Count how many times your path splits.
7. Look into the canopy and notice the color and shape of the leaves. Estimate how many leaves you can actually see and estimate how many the tree may have in total. Imagine a slight breeze making the leaves move and flutter. Can you feel the breeze?
8. Move your focus slowly back until you can see the entire tree from your perspective. Do you know what kind of tree it is?

9. Imagine the tree is growing in reverse, shrinking down as branches and leaves disappear. Once it has shrunk to a seedling, imagine it disappears, leaving only you in the void.

A tree is a great visualization, as most people know this shape well. It doesn't matter which kind of tree it is, but the more complex, the better. While doing this visualization, you are forcing your mind to recall aspects of trees you have seen in your life and construct one with those attributes.

This is powerful brain entrainment and increases your focus as it increases the power of your imagination. The details are important, and over time, the tree will take on more and more realistic visualizations as you do this exercise. It may be difficult at first, but over time, you will see steady progress until you can visualize incredibly vivid objects as though you are actually seeing them.

Albert Einstein was famous for his visualizations. He claimed to use visualization to imagine chasing after a beam of light. It was an integral part of his process for developing special relativity. Mystics have known for thousands of years our thoughts are powerful creations that under the right circumstances, can be made manifest.

When done correctly, this exercise should take around ten minutes. If you find you are rushing, slow down and think of other details on the tree you can analyze. Creation of something complex should take time to fully imagine. The more effort you put in will equal more focus you get out.

Sensing the Present

Focus isn't just within our imagination, but is also a part of our waking reality. We have five (5) senses to perceive the world, and honing those perceptions is all about focus. Not only will we be more focused and attentive to the world, but our overall thoughts will become more focused and less random.

1. Walk into a room in your home.
2. Scan all the objects visible within the room, counting how many there are.
3. What sounds do you hear? Count and identify as many sounds as you hear.
4. What smells do you detect? Count and identify as many smells as possible.
5. Walk over to an object. Close your eyes and feel the object gently with your fingers. What textures do you feel? Does the feeling evoke an emotion or a memory? Are there multiple touch sensations you feel? What does the boundary from one sensation to the next feel like? Can you visualize the boundary?
6. Lean over or into the object, or pick it up if it is small enough, and with eyes closed, smell it slowly, trying to pick up what scents you can detect. Does it smell pleasant? Is there more than one smell? What does it smell like?
7. Open your eyes and leave the room. Now sit somewhere comfortable, close your eyes and *imagine* you are walking back into the room you just left. Visualize all the objects in their respective places within the room. Notice their color and textures. Do you detect the same smells? Do you hear the same sounds?
8. In your mind's eye, go back to the object you felt before and imagine feeling it again. Does it feel the same? Does it smell the same?
9. When you have a clear visualization of that room and its objects, you may stop.

This exercise may seem frivolous at first glance, but it is an important part of your spiritual journey. You must not only be able to imagine aspects of the world around you, but you must be attentive to the present. How many times have you walked into a room and left remembering nothing about it? You are purposely filtering out the world around you. Live in the present and take in all the sounds, sights, smells and touch you can. When eating, enjoy every flavor and nuance you taste.

There is energy everywhere, not only within. Our sensory systems detect this energy, and to detect that energy is to tune those systems. Many foolishly believe attaining enlightenment is foregoing all sensory stimulations on the physical plane. But enlightenment is experiencing *all* sensorial energies on *all* planes of existence simultaneously. You know the saying, "Stop and smell the roses." You came here for these experiences. Do not ignore them.

Om Japa

This exercise is intended for you to become familiar with your chakras, locate them within your body, and activate them through a simple sound. You will move through the first and fifth chakras going up from the first and then back down from the fifth.

Let's familiarize ourselves one more time with our chakras. The following lists each chakra with its location. If you ever get a chance, have an Aura photo taken to see which of your chakras are the most active within you. It affects who you are and is quite interesting.

1. **Base**: Base of spine near tailbone,
2. **Sacral**: Below belly button above the pubic area,
3. **Solar Plexus**: Upper abdomen near stomach,
4. **Heart**: Center of chest above heart,

5. **Throat**: At throat,
6. **Third Eye**: Center brain behind eyes, and
7. **Crown**: Top of head.

Complete the following steps to master Om Japa and identify your chakras:

1. Sit in meditation.
2. Count up beads.
3. Chant "Ohm" verbally while focusing on your first chakra's location. Feel the vibrations and adjust your focus to locate the sweet spot of the chakra as though tuning a stringed instrument. Draw out the "O" in Ohm before sounding the "m" sound.
4. Repeat the previous step for chakras 2–5. After the fifth chakra, repeat the process again except reversing order moving from the fifth down to the first chakra. You should verbalize the Ohm sound in each chakra for about 2–4 seconds. Going up and back down is one cycle.
5. After completing three cycles, complete three more cycles except sound Ohm mentally rather than verbally.
6. After a month of this, switch to only sounding Ohm mentally.

Again, we are trying to locate each of your chakras, activate them through the Ohm sound, and stimulate energy (prana) to move up and down your etheric channel through these chakras. This is preliminary work for future Kriya Serpent Yoga, so take the time and patience to locate the sweet spot on each chakra. The sweet spot is called the root of the chakra.

Over time, you will feel each chakra open, and then the difference between the sweet spot and just around the sweet spot becomes clearer. Eventually, you will hit the sweet spot with little effort.

You are developing your focus and quieting your monkey mind while doing this exercise. If your mind is truly devoted to this task, it will not have room for other thoughts. If you find your mind wandering at all during this exercise, return your focus and continue the exercise.

It takes time to entrain the grooves of this practice into your mind, so please practice daily as prescribed later in this chapter and with earnest. You will be richly rewarded later in higher levels of Kriya Serpent Yoga.

Deep Breathing

There is a lot written about breathing and dedicated breathing yoga exercises have been developed to improve overall health and spiritual well-being. Of course, we are only concerned with Kriya Serpent Yoga in this book, so we do not delve deep into the yoga of breathing.

However, it is an important part of all yoga practices and integral to Kriya Serpent Yoga. Because of that, we spend some time practicing breath work. Deep Breathing is a simple exercise intended to further develop your breath control for future techniques.

1. Sit in meditation.
2. Count up beads.
3. Inhale through your nose deeply for a count of 8 and then hold the breath for a count of 5.
4. Exhale through your mouth for a count of 8 and then hold for a count of 5.
5. In and out is one cycle so count 1 on your beads before repeating steps 3–5 again until you have completed your total count.

The following are the levels you should achieve with this technique. Start slowly and work your way up:

- **Beginner**: 6 counts,
- **Intermediate**: 12 counts, and
- **Advanced**: 24 counts.

Nadi Shodhana

This technique is part of my daily regimen and will be yours eventually as you move up into the higher levels. For me, it is a way to calm my mind to prepare for meditation, so it is the first exercise I complete in my daily routine.

Nadi Shodhana Pranayama is also known as Alternate Nostril Breathing. It helps clear each side of your nasal cavities to help you breathe better during your regular practice. As I noted above, it begins calming the mind, bringing it into focus for your meditation efforts.

Since you must use one of your hands for alternating a hold on the nostrils, you will use the opposite hand that is not counting (claw back). Using this non-counting hand, you will form a "V" with your fingers by curling your index and middle fingers into your palm while letting your thumb and other fingers extend up and out. This will form a "V" with your hand.

Your thumb and the finger next to your pinky finger will pinch each nostril shut as you alternate. Applying pressure to the outside of your nostril with the finger should be enough to "close" that nostril to inhibit airflow.

You will start with your right side nostril first, so press your finger against it to close it. When you switch, you will simply roll your wrist to open the one side and close the other with the opposite finger.

1. Sit in meditation.
2. Count up beads.
3. Close right nostril and inhale through left nostril for a count of 6 or 8. Hold breath for 2 seconds.

4. While holding breath roll your wrist to close left nostril and open the right nostril. Exhale through right nostril for count of 6 or 8. Hold for 2 seconds.
5. Inhale through right nostril for count of 6 or 8. Hold breath for 2 seconds.
6. While holding breath, roll your wrist to close the right nostril and open the left nostril. Exhale through left nostril for count of 6 or 8. Hold for 2 seconds.
7. Inhale through left nostril for count of 6 or 8. Hold breath for 2 seconds.
8. You have completed one cycle of this breathing so count 1 on beads. Return to step 4 and repeat through step 7 until you have completed total counts.

The following are the levels you should achieve with this technique. Start slowly and work your way up:

- **Beginner**: 3 cycles,
- **Intermediate**: 6 cycles, and
- **Advanced**: 12 cycles.

The key here is to ensure your inhalation and exhalation counts are identical. If you have trouble breathing, count 6, but if you are fine doing it longer, then count 8. Some have recommended a count of 10, but for my practice, that seems long and makes it too much of a chore. I am older, so shorter breathing is a natural consequence of that. Adjust based on your own body, but make sure in and out are the same count.

Kriya Serpent Techniques

Since this is the introductory level, it is assumed you will not raise your Kundalini yet. That doesn't mean it can't happen, but it is not likely. However, this is the start of your Kriya

Serpent journey. The following technique is what you did in the test earlier. The goal is to learn the sounds of Kriya Serpent so you can internalize the vocalization, visualizing it precisely as practiced here. The sound is *important*, even when only mentally intoning.

Let's look again at the Kriya Serpent symbols, sounds and meanings:

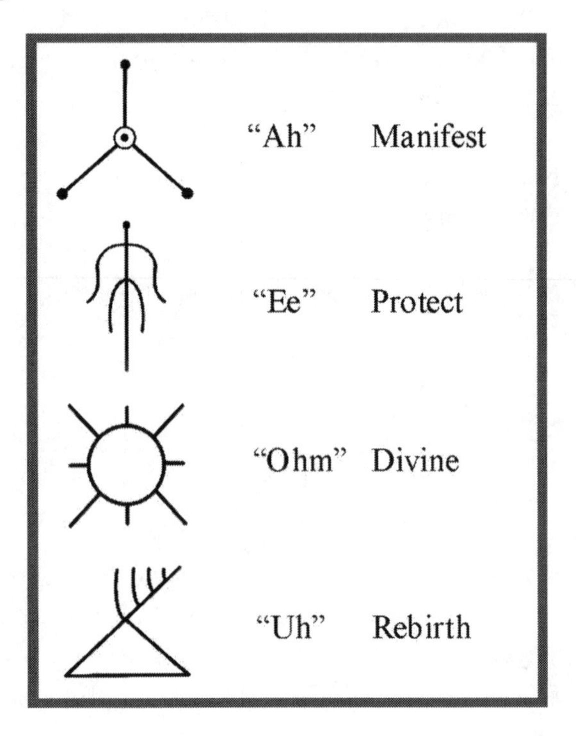

In this technique, we want to experience all the symbols by intoning the sound verbally while mentally visualizing the symbol and its meaning.

1. Sit in meditation.
2. Count up beads.
3. Inhale through your nose slowly.

4. Exhale as you intone the symbol's sound verbally while picturing the symbol and its meaning. Intone a consistent sound as long as you have breath. Return to step three and repeat, doing it once for each symbol in the following order:
    - Ah,
    - Ee,
    - Ohm, and
    - Uh.
5. Once you do all four (4) sounds, you have completed one cycle. Count up one on your beads and repeat steps 3 and 4 until you have completed your count.

The following are the levels you should achieve with this technique. Start slowly and work your way up:

- **Beginner**: 6 cycles,
- **Intermediate**: 12 cycles, and
- **Advanced**: 24 cycles.

This will energize your body so that the etheric energy flows through you. It is possible this could stimulate your Kundalini, so if it does, do not be shocked or afraid, but allow it to flow up through you and direct it through your crown chakra. Some shaking and muscle tightening is possible if this occurs so do not panic.

It is unlikely this will occur, but I want you to be prepared in the event it does. In the event it does, **stop** practicing immediately once the Kundalini subsides. Since you are not yet prepared for it, it would be prudent for to you discontinue this exercise as it may further stimulate the Kundalini.

I realize you are thinking, but isn't this what we want? Yes, that is our ultimate goal, but if you are not ready, it can be unpleasant and may hold you back spiritually. If it continues every time you use this technique, then you are ready to proceed to the next level after mastering the other techniques within this introductory level.

Daily Regimen

Since this level could take up to 18 months to complete, I want to specify a schedule and timeframe that will accommodate both the very beginning student and those who may pass through these exercises rapidly. I have broken it down into three (3) different phases, each phase working on a specific set of skills. Each phase should take anywhere between 2 to 6 months, longer if you are not advancing quickly. Remember, it is not a race.

While it is possible to interleave these daily regimens together, like every other day or something similar, I truly advise you to complete Phase 1 first, and then you can consider interleaving Phase 2 and Phase 3. Focusing on one phase at a time is the ideal, and I believe it is the best route to go for solid results, but some of you, especially new humans, may find the pace too slow as you see results more rapidly.

Since we are entering the age of the individual, I will leave it to you on how you will approach this. Following my advice is optional, but I really think you will see better results if you do. I get you are impatient, but this takes some time, especially when you are so new to meditation. Start out as I recommend, and see how it goes before deviating later if you choose.

Phase 1: Meditative Stillness (2–6 months)

We must quiet the monkey mind before we can really dive into meditation fully. This first phase is all about that. Every day, sit in meditation and complete the following techniques based on the count/time specified. I have broken it down into 3 different levels, each level taking 2 months to complete if you are new to this.

Use your inner intuition to feel how it is going and see if your results are good enough before moving to the next level. The following is the daily regimen:

Beginner Level Daily Regimen (10 minutes total):

1. Sitting in Meditation: Duration of session,
2. Counting Beads: 12 counts,
3. Focused Breathing: 5 minutes, and
4. Emptiness: 0 minutes.

Intermediate Level Daily Regimen (20 minutes total):

1. Sitting in Meditation: Duration of session,
2. Counting Beads: 36 counts,
3. Focused Breathing: 5 minutes, and
4. Emptiness: 10 minutes.

Advanced Level Daily Regimen (30 minutes total):

1. Sitting in Meditation: Duration of session,
2. Counting Beads: 60 counts,
3. Focused Breathing: 10 minutes, and
4. Emptiness: 15 minutes.

Phase 2: Chakras and Breathing (2–6 months)

In phase 2, we want to identify, locate and activate your main chakras. You will add another breathing technique into your practice and perform each of the visualization techniques once a week. Your goal is to activate your chakras and develop that laser focus you'll need later in this practice. Of course, this implies you have mastered *Phase 1* and quieted your monkey mind.

Beginner Level Daily Regimen (15 minutes total):

1. Sitting in Meditation: Duration of session,
2. Deep Breathing: 6 counts,
3. Nadi Shodhana: 6 counts, and
4. Om Japa: 6 counts.

Intermediate Level Daily Regimen (25 minutes total):

1. Sitting in Meditation: Duration of session,
2. Deep Breathing: 12 counts.
3. Nadi Shodhana: 12 counts, and
4. Om Japa: 12 counts.

Advanced Level Daily Regimen (40 minutes total):

1. Sitting in Meditation: Duration of session,
2. Deep Breathing: 12 counts,
3. Nadi Shodhana: 12 counts, and
4. Om Japa: 24 counts.

As mentioned above, you will integrate the following two exercises into your *weekly* routine (not daily). I find the weekend is perfect for these extra exercises.

1. Visualization: Practice 5–10 minutes during months 1–3, and
2. Sensing the Present: Practice 10–15 minutes months 4–6.

As you begin this phase, it will seem like nothing is really happening, but somewhere between months 2 and 4 you will begin to open your chakras, feeling the energy flow around your body and up through each main chakra.

Your focus exercises may seem difficult at first. If your monkey mind is still chattering, go back and perform the Emptiness exercise before you attempt the focus exercises. Eventually, you will experience more vivid and focused exercises each week.

Phase 3: Kriya Serpent (2–6 months)

If you have followed the long timeline for these phases, you have practiced for one year, the same time I spent studying the Self Realization Fellowship's course. Their lessons had a strong religious focus while developing the meditation techniques. We do not need this religious focus because once you connect to the Divine through Kriya Serpent Yoga, you will have all the religion you need.

This third phase introduces you to Kriya Serpent Yoga. Up to this point, you learned to quiet your monkey mind, sit in meditation, count repetitions with Mala Beads, develop focus through visualization, become more mindful of your present, and activate your main chakras by stimulating energy within your body.

That is a lot, but all are necessary for your spiritual growth. Now, you will learn the sounds, symbols and meanings of Kriya Serpent Yoga, training your mind to visualize the symbols while intoning the sounds. This further stimulates energy within.

Think about it. Since we are all energy and vibrations, stimulating this energetic body with sound and vibrations will build up energy within your energetic body as it flows through your chakras. That is what Kriya Serpent does. Eventually, this ignites the Kundalini within, taking you to higher planes of consciousness.

You will probably change both physically and psychologically in this third phase in ways you may not have expected. This is all positive and prepares you for the next level of this practice. Remain patient and enjoy the experience.

<u>Beginner Level Daily Regimen (10 minutes total):</u>

1. Sitting in Meditation: Duration of session,
2. Nadi Shodhana: 6 counts, and
3. Kriya Serpent: 12 cycles.

<u>Intermediate Level Daily Regimen (20 minutes total):</u>

1. Sitting in Meditation: Duration of session,
2. Nadi Shodhana: 6 counts, and
3. Kriya Serpent: 24 cycles.

<u>Advanced Level Daily Regimen (30 minutes total):</u>

1. Sitting in Meditation: Duration of session,
2. Nadi Shodhana: 6 counts, and
3. Kriya Serpent: 36 cycles.

During this introductory level, we kept the amount of meditation under an hour. For most people, finding the time to do meditation is a battle in our busy lives. In later levels, assume you will spend at least an hour meditating, sometimes longer. Don't worry, with regular practice, you'll be surprised how easy this becomes.

However, fitting it into your daily routine is not so easy. I recommend you do it either early in the morning or before bed. During the day is difficult since you are involved with so many activities and demands. I do my meditation in the early morning as a great way to start my day. Doing it at night, which I sometimes do, is also fantastic as it can lead to remarkable dreams and deep sleep.

The risk of doing it before bed is the threat of falling asleep during the meditation. While sleep can be considered a significant form of meditation, you do not want that to replace your Kriya Serpent practice. Be mindful of what your body tells you and try both times to see which fits better with your lifestyle.

You must be certain to do this every single day. It will be challenging for most early on, but as you progress and begin to experience the power of this practice, you will want to do it every day to gain the benefits it affords you.

Whenever you do it, I must urge you to refrain from consuming stimulants before practice. Being under the influence of such substances deters your progress and slows your evolution. Over time, these cravings will diminish as the energy heals and improves your physical and mental life state.

You still have free will, but exercise it judiciously. Make positive life choices and you will experience positive life states. It is how we were designed to work.

Warnings, Suggestions and Side Effects

At the introductory level, we are not trying to raise the Kundalini, so there are not any serious side effects we have to consider. Having said that, there are a few things I will make a note of:

1. Sitting for long periods in a cross-legged position may put one or more of your *lower extremities to sleep* as blood flow is restricted. I recommend integrating stretching exercises into your routine to adjust for this new position you use daily. If you cannot prevent it, try softer materials for your zabuton or switch to a chair.
2. *Allergies* cause difficult breathing during meditation, and I know having suffered from them most of my life. Use over-the-counter remedies to clear sinuses so you can breathe your best. I use a daily 24-hour spray medication and typically have clear breathing in the mornings because of it. If you are simply too congested, I recommend holding off on your practice until you resume normal breathing.

3. Though it may seem reasonable to meditate while *sick,* I strongly **urge you not to**. Rehabilitate yourself from the illness first before resuming your daily practice.
4. Near the end of this level, you may discover you *need less sleep* than before you started. Keep in mind any good meditation can be viewed as similar to a cycle of sleep as you lower your brainwave patterns into different levels of consciousness. This is normal and welcome as it frees up time to meditate.
5. *Sexual arousal is often stimulated,* especially during Kriya Serpent techniques in the latter part of this level. I recommend easing these urges without resorting to sexual activities. This energy is good and a part of where you are headed. Don't always lower your vibrational state through sexual release. I am not saying don't have sex. I am saying don't always do it after your meditation. You don't want to entrain yourself with that association, as it will lead to troubling problems down the road.

The Next Level

Once you have achieved the Advanced mastery levels in each of the three phases of Level 1, you will be ready to move onto Level 2. As mentioned before, it is important to master these techniques and train your body and mind for the mindfulness of meditation. You are laying the foundation of your future practice at this level and want to ensure it is solid before you take the next steps.

While the expectations are flexible, you really have to determine when and if you have achieved the results before moving on. In the latter levels of Kriya Serpent Yoga, you will develop your inner guru, who will lead you down the path as a regular guru would. It is a rather remarkable thing and part of the new age that is coming.

However, in these early stages, that inner voice is not developed, but you still have intuition. The best judge of you is you. Pay close attention to the physical feelings you experience in this practice, and your body's changes will lead you to the next stages.

If you believe you are ready to move on, then your Kriya Serpent technique, which is like the test at the beginning, should have stimulated far more within you than the very first time you took the test. Keep track of these and see where you fall based on the results of the test.

While for some, it may show a much higher level, if you started here, continue the linear path through the book from one level to the next. If you are more advanced, you will fly through the lower levels quickly.

More than anything, rejoice in the beginning of a lifetime practice that will take you on a journey you can barely even imagine during these early stages. The Universe is a mysterious and magical place that offers more than we know or are prepared to accept. We are training you to be prepared for this unveiling so you benefit from all the Universe offers.

Chapter 7

Each morning, we are born again. What we do today is what matters most.
Buddha

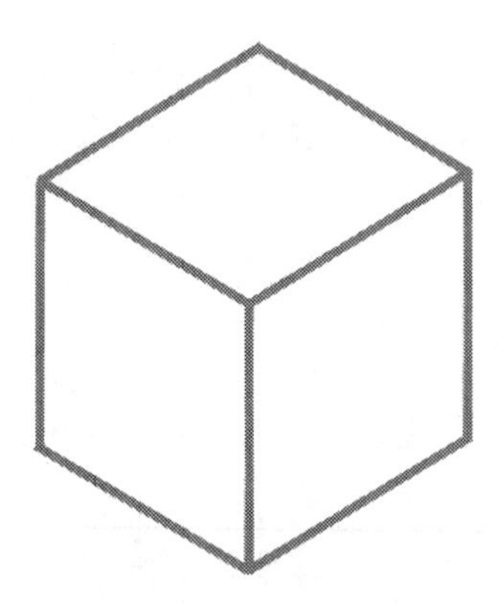

Beginner Level 2

Introduction

Congratulations, you are about to start the full Kriya Serpent Yoga practice. We need to develop a few more skills before we get you on the ground running, but they do not take too long. It is important you are familiar with and mastered the techniques of Level 1. If you have not mastered Level 1 skills, please go back and complete everything on Level 1 before starting here.

Having said this, if you tested into this level, you are ready to start the fundamental practice of Kriya Serpent Yoga. However, you may not have mastered all the required skills. Review the Introductory Level 1 objective skills and complete any you need to master.

On this level, we add another breathing technique and introduce you to a technique similar to Om Japa. It will move energy up and down your etheric channels to stimulate your chakras. The purpose is to hone your control of the etheric energy of Kriya Serpent Yoga. If you control the energy, you control your evolution.

On this level, the Kriya Serpent technique you'll learn is the basic technique I was taught and is the basis for all practices beyond this level. On the higher levels, you'll learn variations to this initial technique, increasing your vibrational energy. High vibrational energy is important for achieving the higher states of consciousness necessary to connect with the Divine.

But let's not get ahead of ourselves. This initial Kriya Serpent technique is called *The Song of the Serpent*. In essence, you will entice the Kundalini (energy serpent within) to rise through your main chakras. It is called a song because we are intoning the sounds of the symbols of Kriya Serpent, just like a song.

The assumption is you have already done this and learned the symbols and sounds in the previous level. If not, **STOP** and **GO BACK** to that earlier technique before moving on. Keep in mind, our goal in Level 2 is to activate the Kundalini within you, so your body, emotions and mind must be fully prepared to handle this surge.

Everything on Level 1 prepared you for Kundalini, so be sure you mastered those earlier skills. I realize some come into this with significant meditation and yogic experience, and if this is you, proceed onward. But for those without the requisite skills, this can be hazardous.

Use your best judgment, and if it tells you to proceed, move on. We will look at the objective skills we wish to accomplish in this Beginner Level 2.

Objective Skills

1. **Sit in meditation**: We master this skill and extend meditation time. *Mastery* is achieved when you can sit comfortably without moving or discomfort for the entirety of your session.

2. **Counting beads**: This is fundamental to all our practices. *Mastery* is using Mala beads to count all repetitions.
3. **Breath control**: You will learn a new breathing technique. *Mastery* is when you easily perform this breathing technique.
4. **Moving Energy though Chakras**: You will use mental focus to channel energy (prana) through the main chakras. *Mastery* is attained when you can stimulate each chakra.
5. **Song of the Serpent**: The basis for all Kriya Serpent techniques. *Mastery* is when you can intone all the sounds while visualizing the associated symbols.
6. **Meditating**: Sit in stillness after all techniques completed. Mastery is when you achieve altered states of consciousness and stillness of thought.

Breathe Control

You will continue your breath training by learning a new technique. We will still use some older techniques learned on Level 1, but eventually, those will be replaced. The following is the new technique you will learn.

1. **Ujjayi Breathing**: You will perform this technique with various counts. This is a very common breathing technique in many types of yoga.

Energy Control in Chakras

You have located and chanted into your main chakras, but we now want to extend that to moving etheric energy (prana) up and down these chakras. It is all about focus. Our goal with energy control is to move it up and down our etheric energy channel through our chakras. This not only has positive impacts on balancing our chakras, but it will later help us activate the Kundalini.

1. **Pranayama**: You will perform this technique with various counts. This technique was borrowed from Kriya Yoga.
2. **Song of the Serpent**: You will perform this technique with various counts. This technique is the basis of Kriya Serpent Yoga.

Meditating

As you practice the true Kriya Serpent Yoga, you must meditate after completing all the techniques. On Beginner Level 2, you will focus on stillness, noting the sensations in both mind and body. On the higher levels, this meditation time will be filled with many spiritual things, but for now, we must calm the mind and find stillness.

Traditional Techniques

Ujjayi Breathing

I still use this technique in my daily practice for good reason. It calms my mind and body, allowing me to sharpen my focus and visualization. On higher levels, it can activate your Kundalini. It is doubtful you will activate the Kundalini while doing Ujjayi Breathing this early in your practice.

However, when you practice frequently, your body is conditioned to the Kundalini, and it can rise outside the techniques designed to activate it. I even experience Kundalini while at work, but that is another story entirely.

Ujjayi Breathing will calm the mind to prepare you for the *Pranayama* or *Song of the Serpent* technique. But before I outline this simple technique, you must first understand the difference between it and ordinary breathing.

In Ujjayi Breathing, you restrict the throat slightly. When I was first learning it, I was confused, so I went online to look up videos about it. I found one that gave me the best advice to learn this throat restriction.

Remember, as a kid, when you would breathe on a cold window pane and write something in the condensation? Well, the way you breathed on that cold window is the same restriction in your throat you use for Ujjayi Breathing. Try it out.

When we blow out to cause the condensation, we naturally restrict our throat to ensure the breath coming out is the warmest possible. Same principle applies here. We want our breath to be restricted to create a warmer breath than we might ordinarily have.

Now, try to inhale using that same restriction as in your exhalation. Can you see how your throat is restricted slightly as you inhale and exhale? That is the breathing you need for this exercise. You only need a slight restriction, like you would when steaming a window, so don't overdo it and hurt your throat or cause discomfort.

1. Sit in meditation.
2. Count up beads.
3. Inhale with restricted throat. While inhaling, listen to the sound the air makes as it passes through the restriction. It sounds similar to water rushing off the beach as it builds into another wave. Visualize this water running back from the beach to the next wave.
4. Exhale with restricted throat. Pay attention to the sound of the air as it exits through the restricted throat. It sounds similar to the crash of a wave on the beach. This is why this technique is often called *Ocean Breathing*. Visualize this water crashing onto the beach as you exhale.
5. You have completed one cycle, so count down one bead.
6. Repeat steps 3–5 until you have completed your total count.

The following are the levels you should achieve with this technique. Start slowly and work your way up:

- **Beginner**: 12 cycles,
- **Intermediate**: 24 cycles, and
- **Advanced**: 36 cycles.

Pranayama

You will build on the Om Japa technique, moving the energy from the Base chakra into your Third Eye chakra and then back down again. The difference here is that you already know where each chakra is located and you want to do this in a *single* inhalation and exhalation. This makes it a speedier process than Om Japa, and therefore, you will do more counts.

1. Sit in meditation.
2. Count up beads.
3. Inhale and chant Ohm mentally in each of the following chakras, moving your focus from one to the next as you move your focus up during the inhalation. Pause after the Third Eye chakra for 2 seconds:
    - Base,
    - Sacral,
    - Solar Plexus,
    - Heart,
    - Throat, and
    - Third Eye.
4. Exhale and chant Ohm mentally in each of the following chakras, moving your focus from one to the next as you move your focus down during the exhalation. Pause after Base chakra for 2 seconds:
    - Third Eye,
    - Throat,
    - Heart,
    - Solar Plexus,
    - Sacral, and
    - Base.

5. On inhalation you are moving up, and on exhalation you are moving down through the chakras, transferring the energy up and down the etheric channel through each chakra. Moving up and then down is one cycle, so count one bead.
6. Repeat steps 3 through 5 until you have completed your total count.
7. If your Kundalini rises, direct it through your Crown chakra.

The following are the levels you should achieve with this technique. Start slowly and work your way up:

- **Beginner**: 12 cycles,
- **Intermediate**: 24 cycles, and
- **Advanced**: 48 cycles.

When I practiced Pranayama, I chanted the three lower chakras and then the three upper chakras, for a total count of six. I used a two count of three Ohms. Once you add this to your daily regimen, you will understand what I mean by the 2-three cadence:

Ohm, ohm, ohm—ohm, ohm, ohm

Pranayama is a valuable skill. You will eventually replace it with the Kriya Serpent technique, but mastery of this first skill is critical. I always enjoyed this technique, though I no longer practice it. However, I reviewed it again before publishing, and it is still wonderful.

So, you must master Pranayama before moving on. Using focus to move energy through your etheric channel is fundamental to the Kriya Serpent technique. This will probably activate your Kundalini, so be prepared for that to happen. It was the technique I was using when I had my first Kundalini experience.

Later on, the Kriya Serpent technique activates Kundalini continuously, but this technique typically takes longer. As a reminder, your goal is to raise the Kundalini (a lot), connect with the Divine and find your purpose. Never lose sight of that, because this practice was designed for that primary goal.

On the higher levels, you'll learn how Kundalini helps with your purpose, so you need its activation even after you discover your purpose.

Kriya Serpent Techniques

Song of the Serpent

Song of the Serpent was the first daily practice I used after learning Kriya Serpent, and it will stimulate your Kundalini while increasing overall energy flow through your etheric body. Follow the directions exactly, and you will begin your journey on the path of the Kriya Serpent Yogi.

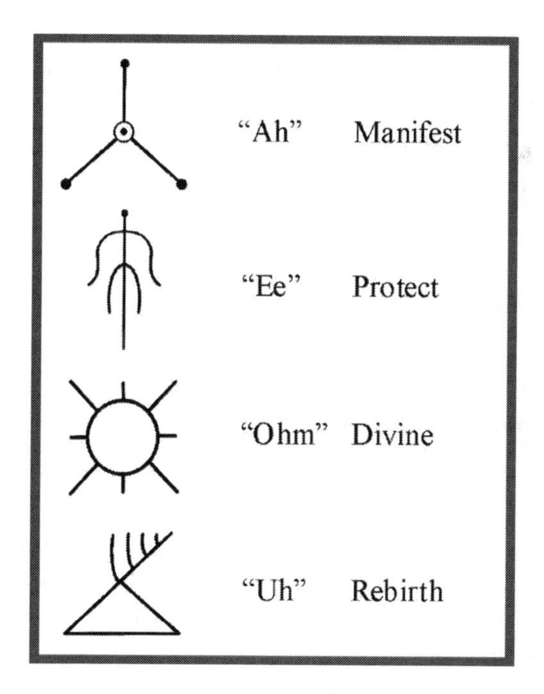

I listed the Kriya Serpent symbols, sounds and meanings again as a reminder for this practice. Just like in Introductory Level 1, this technique requires you to chant the sounds while visualizing the symbols. However, unlike that earlier technique you will chant with 2 breaths instead of 4 in the earlier technique.

1. Sit in meditation.
2. Count up beads.
3. **Inhale** and mentally chant "Ah" into your Heart chakra while visualizing the *Manifest* symbol.
4. **Exhale** and mentally chant "Ee" into your Heart chakra while visualizing the *Protect* symbol.
5. **Inhale** and mentally chant "Ohm" into your Heart chakra while visualizing the Divine symbol.
6. **Exhale** and mentally chant "Uh" into your Heart chakra while visualizing the *Rebirth* symbol.
7. You have completed 1 cycle of this technique, so count down 1 bead.
8. Repeat steps 3–7 until you have completed your total count.
9. If the Kundalini rises, DO NOT direct it into your Heart chakra but through your *Crown chakra*. **This is important!**

The following are the levels you should achieve with this technique. Start slowly and work your way up:

- **Beginner**: 12 cycles,
- **Intermediate**: 24 cycles, and
- **Advanced**: 36 cycles.

There are a few key points to make here. First, when you inhale, inhale up into your chest as opposed to your belly. In many yoga techniques, they instruct you to breathe into your belly, but for Kriya Serpent, we always want to breathe into our chest.

This will help raise the Kundalini as we activate our spinal muscles for that eventuality.

Second, it is very important that you breathe into your Heart chakra for this technique. I questioned this myself as I imagined it would be more like the Pranayama technique passing through all the main chakras into the Third Eye chakra and then back down. I was told this beginning technique through the Heart chakra is intended to help develop love and compassion for all living beings.

If our purpose is to usher in the next evolutionary stage of humanity, then love and compassion are critical for us to develop. Otherwise, we are no better than the Homo sapiens who still focus their love on themselves as opposed to other humans and other beings.

Everything you see and experience is created by the Divine, therefore, it is Divine in nature. How can you not love and have compassion for anything that is Divine? It is our delusion, hubris and ignorance that makes us so heartless with each other, to our planet and to all the life on this planet. We lack the proper understanding and knowledge to see this, but our Kriya Serpent practice will change that.

My last point is that when I practiced this technique, my Kundalini activated on nearly every final exhalation within a cycle while chanting "Uh" for the Rebirth Symbol. Later, the Kundalini activated during both exhalations.

This is the power of Kriya Serpent Yoga, a direct activation of Kundalini through a simple to learn and easy-to-use technique. If you are a new human, your Kundalini will activate using this technique. It is the purpose of its revival during the end of the Age of Pisces.

As mentioned before, we direct the Kundalini through our Crown chakra. As necessity would dictate to reach the Crown chakra, your Kundalini will flow up through your etheric channel and through all your main chakras. *This is what you want to happen!* As you raise your Kundalini more often through the Crown chakra, you will experience a change in your state of consciousness, as though someone is opening a new door in your mind.

It will energize you and cause a lot of heat to build along your spinal muscles and within your head. This is normal, so if you start the practice cold, know that you will become hot. Do not dress too warm or you will need to strip off layers, interrupting your practice and losing that altered state of consciousness. Remember, you will sit on a wool blanket, so being slightly chilly at the start is fine.

Meditating

Assuming you have completed all the techniques correctly, you will now be in an altered state of consciousness. In terms of your brain waves, you will no longer be in Beta waves (normal waking), and are likely shifting into Alpha wave patterns, a more relaxed state of mind more akin to a light sleep. But do not fall asleep. If you do, it isn't the end of the world, but make sure you meditate at a time when you are less likely to fall asleep.

1. After completing the last technique of your regimen, twist your beads once and place your middle fingers into the two formed loops, bringing them together, interlacing your fingers. Place your hands in your lap.
2. Remain absolutely still and breathe slowly in and out, pausing for 2 seconds between inhalations and exhalations.
3. As you inhale, mentally chant "Hang" (sounds like *song* with a hard "a").
4. As you exhale, mentally chant "Sau" (sounds like saw).
5. Hold the chant for the entirety of each breath.

This chanting further slows your mind and body as you relax. *Visualize* being inside a gray sphere, drifting further into a deeper state of consciousness. At this stage, you have neither an agenda nor a mission to accomplish. Let your mind sink into a deeper state of consciousness. For me, I feel like I am floating into a dark, warm void.

Later, things will happen during this stage, but for now, the stillness and deep states of consciousness are the only goal. Focus on the gray sphere while chanting and you will find the stillness within. If the gray sphere turns into a black void, this is perfectly fine. Just let it happen as you sink deeper.

At this point, you have activated each chakra, run Kundalini through them, slowed your heart rate and brain waves, and entered into altered states of consciousness. This attunes your body and mind to the energies of the Universe, and these energies connect you with the Divine so you can discover your purpose. With this practice, you raise your overall vibrational state, activating your Siddhis while unlocking dormant DNA.

I cannot overstate the power of this practice. You will notice the effects immediately. It is everything Paramahansa Yogananda said it was when he taught Kriya Yoga. However, with Kriya Serpent Yoga, you advance rapidly while developing love for everything. You will see beauty everywhere, increasing your life state and happiness.

However, there is one more thing you need to add to your meditation practice: *prayer*. Many prefer to add prayer at the beginning of the meditating stage, while others add it at the end of the overall session. Either way, it is an important part of this practice. For some, this may be entirely new to you, and that is fine. For others, you may have been raised like me in a more traditional religious background, where prayer was a common practice.

It is easy, and if you want to connect to the Divine, then you better start by saying "Hello" and "Thank you." Your prayers should focus on showing gratitude for everything in your world. Here is a list of things I show gratitude for:

- My very existence,
- My purpose (even if you have yet to receive it),
- My family, friends and co-workers,
- My job, home and wealth,
- My body, mind and health, and
- My meditation practice.

You get the idea. I also add in how much I love the Divine and the love that It gives back to me. Though it may surprise you, at some point, you will feel the Divine love in a physical way. I liken it to a warm shower of happiness tingling throughout your body. It will probably make you cry the first time you experience it. Some call this sensation a state of bliss, though it is short-term bliss.

You will realize you are loved and important to the Divine, and that is worth getting *emotional* about. Every time I feel that shower of love, I am still surprised. It is truly amazing and keeps you coming back for more.

Beginner Level 2 will give you experiences you could only dream about. It is quite remarkable as you seek your purpose in this lifetime. Welcome to the world of Kriya Serpent Yoga, your path to spiritual evolution and reconnecting with your Creator.

Daily Regimen

As in the previous level, Beginner Level 2 is broken into different phases, each with a specific daily regimen. The overall level should take between 4–12 months depending on your spiritual progress and prior experiences. The key on this level is to achieve **Kundalini**. For many, this will be their first time, but until that happens, maintain a daily practice before moving onward.

Phase 1: Pranayama (2–6 months)
In Phase 1, you will activate your chakras while moving energy through your physical and etheric bodies to prepare for Kundalini. Your overall time in meditation will increase during this phase:

<u>Beginner Level Daily Regimen (30 minutes total):</u>

1. Sitting in Meditation: Duration of session,
2. Nadi Shodhana: 6 counts,
3. Ujjayi Breathing: 6 counts,
4. Pranayama: 12 cycles, and
5. Meditating: 15 minutes.

<u>Intermediate Level Daily Regimen (40 minutes total):</u>

1. Sitting in Meditation: Duration of session,
2. Nadi Shodhana: 12 counts,
3. Ujjayi Breathing: 12 counts,
4. Pranayama: 24 cycles, and
5. Meditating: 15 minutes.

<u>Advanced Level Daily Regimen (60 minutes total):</u>

1. Sitting in Meditation: Duration of session,
2. Nadi Shodhana: 12 counts,
3. Ujjayi Breathing: 24 counts,
4. Pranayama: 48 cycles, and
5. Meditating: 15 minutes.

In the beginning, 30 minutes may be challenging, especially if you spent little time on Level 1. This is okay, so don't get frustrated if the mind refuses to sink into slower brainwave patterns. For some, they may feel energized and ready for the day as the energy flows through them. This is normal, but over time, your body will adjust and your mind will slow down. Then, you will enter deeper states.

Something similar may occur when you first encounter Kundalini. It is a powerful force and will raise your overall energy tremendously, thus making it difficult to meditate for 15 minutes afterwards. This too shall pass, so be patient and continue practicing daily. You will adjust to the experiences and eventually get that peaceful stillness we are looking for.

Once your Kundalini has risen 3–4 times, you are ready to move on to the next phase. However, pay attention to the side effects before you make that decision. If the Kundalini side effects are fairly intense and you feel a lot of anxiety, do not move on as Kriya Serpent will be even more intense. Stay in Pranayama until the intensity subsides. Again, you should not be in a hurry, but give your body and mind time to adjust to this new etheric you.

Phase 2: Song of the Serpent (2–6 months)

In this phase, you are really trying to raise your Kundalini every single day during your practice. If you are a new human or have had a lot of success with Kundalini in the past, you will raise it every time without a problem.

As mentioned in Phase 1, if the intensity of the Kundalini is too much, hold off on this, or alternate between days doing Phase 1 and Phase 2 interleaved. This will lessen the intensity but allow you to move onward through this level. I cannot stress enough how intense Kundalini can feel initially, so take your time.

Eventually, it will be a daily dose you look forward to. In fact, when I break for a day or two because of life circumstances, I don't feel quite right. A sign of addiction perhaps, but an addiction I will thrive with.

Beginner Level Daily Regimen (30 minutes total):

1. Sitting in Meditation: Duration of session,
2. Nadi Shodhana: 6 counts,
3. Ujjayi Breathing: 6 counts,
4. Song of the Serpent: 12 cycles, and
5. Meditating: 15 minutes.

Intermediate Level Daily Regimen (40 minutes total):

1. Sitting in Meditation: Duration of session,
2. Nadi Sodhana: 6 counts,
3. Ujjayi Breathing: 12 counts,
4. Song of the Serpent: 24 cycles, and
5. Meditating: 20 minutes.

Advanced Level Daily Regimen (60 minutes total):

1. Sitting in Meditation: Duration of session,
2. Nadi Shodhana: 6 counts,
3. Ujjayi Breathing: 12 counts,
4. Song of the Serpent: 36 cycles, and
5. Meditating: 30 minutes.

Keep in mind the time I have listed is approximate, and as you get better at each technique, you will find the estimate is probably too much time. Either way, when you are advanced, you will sit 1–2 times daily for 60 minutes each.

In my practice, I sit once daily for 60–90 minutes each morning. You find that the busier your life, the more difficult it is to sit twice a day. By the time evening rolls around, I am too tired from a full day, and meditation just isn't practical, as I will probably fall asleep. Instead, I practice Mystical Energy techniques before bed, but that is detailed in a subsequent book. Again, if you are too tired, please go to bed and meditate in the morning or another day.

You should experience Kundalini during Song of the Serpent. I mean a lot of Kundalini. For me, the Kundalini rises on nearly every exhalation at the end of the cycle when I am mentally chanting "Uh." This is the Rebirth symbol of Kriya Serpent, and if I had to pick when the Kundalini would rise, it would be during Rebirth.

We are reborn, or at least remade into a better version of ourselves. This entire practice corrects many wrongs that have occurred during your life because of your conditioning and ego. You are releasing negative karma and burning it, thus being reborn with a clean slate.

Kundalini rises within me during the exhalation of "Ee," or Protect, and this makes sense as Kundalini protects you from health and spiritual problems. There is more on this in later books, but for now, know there is an *inherent* protection from this yoga.

Occasionally, the Kundalini rises during inhalations, but this is rare. There are days when the energy is almost explosive, and you might feel the Kundalini rise within an inhalation or during earlier techniques like Ujjayi Breathing. This is normal, so do not freak out.

You may be tempted to hold the Kundalini back while it is very energetic and flowing continuously. DO NOT hold it back! Go with the flow or you may create blockages which you do not want. Think about it. If it is flowing a lot, it is because you need it to. I found when my negative karma resurfaced, the Kundalini worked overtime to burn it away (more on this in the next section).

As before, direct the Kundalini through your Crown chakra. You may experience the following things when the Kundalini flows through you:

- Increased heat in your body, especially the spine and head,
- Shaking throughout your body,
- Core muscles contracting,
- Head pushing back as if trying to straighten your spine,
- Sinuous rocking forward and backward as though a current is flowing through you (because it is),
- Pressure in your head,
- Inability to inhale while energy is flowing, or
- All muscles contracting at once.

Your experiences will probably differ from mine. That is fine, but don't be afraid or stop unless it is simply too intense. If it is too intense, **stop** meditating and take a break for a day or two before restarting. Each day can be different as your physical, emotional and psychological conditions impact your practice in ways you can't predict.

Before I end this Phase 2 section, I want you to consider something. Each day when you sit to meditate, look at what the start time is and what the end time is. If you have a watch or other device to time it directly, great, as long as these devices do not interfere with your session.

At some point, you will experience *mental* interruptions when you reach the desired time (60 minutes). It will feel as though an alarm goes off in your mind. This is conditioning, and once you experience that, it marks significant progress. It will also get you to work on time.

There may be times when you get that inner alarm, but do not wish to stop because of the incredible state of consciousness you are experiencing. Later in your practice, when you do things besides meditating in stillness, you will want to continue your session for as long as the experiences are occurring. This is okay as long as you do not have to catch a bus or be at work at a specific start time (like me), etc.

If you meditate in the evening, then you can go as long as you want as long as you are not falling asleep. I have been involved in some very intense and remarkable experiences in my meditation, which kept me going well beyond the 60-minute mark. The longest I have ever sat in one session was 105 minutes, and I didn't want to stop even then.

However, what I was involved in (and who with) urged me to stop and get on with my day. I complied, but was in such an intense state of bliss that I really didn't want to stop. It becomes very magical, and you will crave it.

Warnings, Suggestions and Side Effects

The following are things you may experience while practicing the Song of the Serpent. This list is probably not complete, as some more advanced experiences have been placed within Intermediate Level 3. You will probably experience far more in the later levels than in this initial practice. However, once the Kundalini rises regularly, things happen.

Do not feel you are a failure if you do not experience all or any of these things because it isn't expected yet. However, if you are a new human, some of these and more may manifest during your meditations, so don't be surprised or fearful.

1. *Acute anxiety* is the most common side effect many experience with Kundalini. Having suffered from anxiety for a long time, I know how uncomfortable this is. Try grounding techniques if it gets too bad:
    - Warm shower or bath.
    - Grounding crystals.
    - Walking outside without shoes or socks in the grass, sand, or dirt.
    - Intense exercise like running, biking, yoga, weights, or anything that pushes your muscles to exhaustion.

- Listening to spa/meditation/nature music. I love sounds of nature when I am stressed because it reconnects me with Gaia.

2. *Surfacing negative karma.* This can manifest as visions or memories of some of the worst times in your life. You may feel ashamed by your previous actions and it may make you feel bad about yourself. DO NOT take any actions to resolve such karma with the people who were affected by your actions. You are not ready for advanced processing and may cause more harm than good to you and to others. For now, let these memories surface, process them by yourself and trust the Kundalini to burn them from your Soul.
3. *Surfacing past traumas.* These are the worst, since most of us have suppressed them. This suppression causes so much grief in our lives that the Kundalini has no choice but to force you to relive it as part of your spiritual growth and healing. It is challenging, but the positive effects of the Kundalini help lessen the sting of reliving such things. If you need to, seek professional counseling. They have many techniques to help you process this trauma and free yourself from its grip on your psyche.
4. *Internal religious visions.* As you are just starting, be wary of what you see. If it is persistent, like an enlightened being reaching out to you, welcome them. However, tell them you are new to this practice and want to gain more experience before communicating with others (more in later chapters). If you see visions of your purpose, document all you see after your meditation is over.
5. *Activation of Siddhis.* Yes, this is possible. You may have visions of things that have not yet happened. Perhaps you'll notice you can almost hear others thinking. Likely, your intuition will be more in tune with your surroundings,

and you may know something before it happens. Observe these but do not pursue them just yet. If you are currently educating yourself about these phenomena, then practice them as if they are part of this education, but if not, stay focused on your meditation practice for now.

6. *Mental downloads*. These are information flowing into your mind about subjects you were not thinking about or interested in. This is your mind connecting with and receiving information from the *Akashic Records*. Learn all that comes to you, but double check things with alternative (more traditional) sources before acting on the information. Like you would when you learn something on the Internet.
7. *Psychotic break*. This is very rare but can be a life-changing event if it happens. It typically presents as a mental explosion of your reality, your life, your beliefs and your current circumstances. With the legalization of marijuana around the United States, this is happening to many people who abuse it. If this happens, hang on to your core self and beliefs, knowing you will survive and carry on. If you have firm beliefs in deities or significant religious personages, then please reach out to them and ask for help. Think about them as being a rock to cling to while you are being swept away by a torrential river. Seek professional help if you need to.
8. *Vivid and Lucid Dreams*. These are normal if you experience them. My dreams became quite vivid, and I found I slept much better than I had before the practice. Lucid dreams were new to me, but I love them. In mine, I have a specific spirit guide (I call them Avatars) whom I learn from. For many people, it is a fantastic journey into a world you create. If you meet a spirit guide while in your lucid dream, please listen to what they tell you because they are there to help you grow spiritually. While developing

more advanced techniques of Kriya Serpent, I stumbled upon a meditation whereby I can enter the dream state and then become lucid. Incredible, but not fully developed. Perhaps this will be something for the future!

9. *Changes in your lifestyle*. Okay, this is one of those things everyone wants to pounce upon as "cultish," but it is quite the contrary. Neither I nor anyone else associated with Kriya Serpent Yoga will ever tell you how to live your life. That is entirely up to you. However, as you practice, you will find your choices will change. I gave up smoking cigars, increased my workout regimen and stopped drinking alcohol. Not because I "thought" it was the right thing to do, but because it is what my mind and body were telling me to do. You may find the same thing. For some, this might cause distress as they cling to their past behaviors and conditioning. Do what feels right to you. I certainly do not judge anyone.
10. *Changes in your personality*. Those same people will pounce again, but this really is all you. A spiritual awakening is a very major life event that will change you profoundly. You will not be a different person, but you will be a more enlightened, more compassionate and more intuitive person who suddenly finds others gravitating towards them. You will be happier and look at life through fresh eyes.
11. *Memories of past lives*. This can be disconcerting as not all past lives are filled with wonderful experiences or a wonderful us. Yes, we have all done bad things somewhere down the line, and it usually corresponds with the era we are remembering. Embrace these memories and use them to grow spiritually. I believe we only remember those lives that we need to learn from to help in this current incarnation. Think about what you can learn from that past life, and try to integrate that knowledge into your

practice and spiritual growth. Once you remember past lives, you will no longer fear death.

12. *State of bliss or experiencing unconditional love.* These things are not a daily occurrence, but they can occur from time to time. It is far more likely that they will occur in later stages of your spiritual growth, but if they happen now, enjoy them and take them for what they are, the love of your Creator.

The Next Level

If your Kundalini has not risen, you are not ready to move on. In fact, if you haven't experienced it, you may not be a new human or may be early in your spiritual journey. Do not be discouraged by this, but continue to practice and wait for your Soul and body to determine when you are prepared.

If you are not ready, you are not ready, and there is little you can do other than to continue the practice to condition your etheric system to handle the eventual energy flow. In the meantime, you will grow in many other ways, and your time will not be wasted. Each daily practice is as important as the one before or the one after, so do not stop because you do not progress at the speeds I have outlined within this chapter. Your time will come.

If, however, you have experienced a great deal of Kundalini and believe you have adapted to it well, then you are ready to move on. Though not everyone will receive a sign from an internal guru, this may happen to you. This is how I knew to continue since I was the only one using this yoga at the time of this writing.

An internal guru is something you will experience eventually, some sooner than others. When it occurs, embrace it as your Soul speaking to you with wisdom from all your previous lives. Mine has not only told me when to move on, but how to move on as well. Each new technique is a gift from my inner guru and spirit guides, helping me to bring this new yoga back into the world for all the new humans.

But fear not. If you have no inner guru yet, they will appear eventually. Until then, listen to your body and your mind. Is the Kundalini still causing a lot of side effects you consider disturbing? If so, do not move on. Is the Kundalini flowing freely and your reactions to it positive and uplifting? Then maybe you should move on.

There is no detriment to staying at this level if you feel this is all still too new and you need more experience. This is not a race, but a spiritual growth that will take as long as it takes. In the meantime, you will enjoy all the goodness of this new connection to Universal energies.

From a spiritual standpoint, we hope to connect with the Divine and learn our purpose in this lifetime. If you feel you have connected with the Divine, then you are ready for the next level. If you find that you have contact with other Celestial entities each time you meditate, then you are likely ready to move on.

Intermediate Level 3, is all about our purpose and the connection to the Divine. The yoga techniques are not significantly different from this level, but our focus and the time we spend meditating shifts dramatically.

Level 3 will expand your understanding of the Universe, the Divine and your role within this reality. If you feel prepared for that, move onward, but if you are hesitant, wait until you are ready. The next level will always be there when you are ready to take that plunge into the unknown.

Chapter 8

Yoga is a light, which once lit will never dim. The better your practice, the brighter your flame.
B.K.S. Iyengar

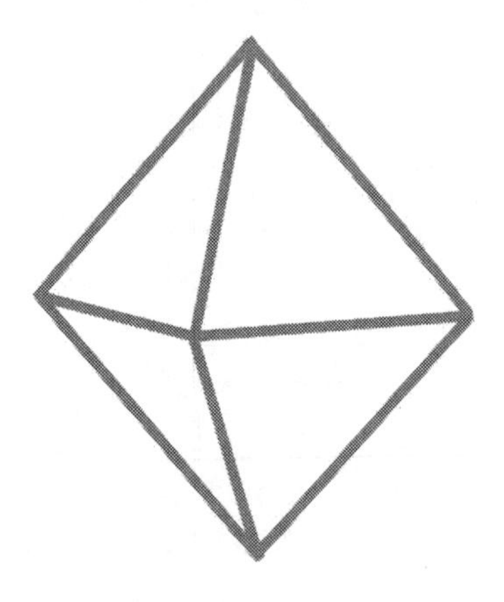

Intermediate Level 3

Introduction

Welcome to the next stage in your evolution. Up to this point, you have learned the basics of yoga meditation, enhancing your techniques while moving higher in the practice. Eventually, you experienced Kundalini, and it altered you in ways you probably had not imagined.

You are here because you are ready to expand your practice and begin your focus on your purpose to serve the Divine. Yes, that is what this is all about: to serve the Divine. Let me expand again on this concept of the Divine because, at this stage, you need to understand what this reality is about.

Though I touched upon this earlier, it is good to narrow our focus. I will not present a biblical diatribe about earth and humanity, or all the celestial or galactic entities involved in it.

There are hundreds of books, including the Bible, which outline these in excruciating detail. These external concepts should always be a part of your continuing education, and the final chapter of this book contains resources to assist you.

What I want to do now is ask you some questions. The answers you give will determine your trajectory. First, assuming you believe our Universe is the product of intelligent design, would you want to help that intelligence with humanity's evolution? If God came down and asked you point blank "I need you to do this..." would you do it?

Do not offer a glib answer, or answer in a way you think I might like. This is you working for the Creator of our Universe. Would you help? In the world of new age thinkers, there is a saying that few are called, but even fewer answer the call. If you are called, would you answer?

Unpack this for a moment. It is a very large reality packed into a tiny amount of words, yet it is so powerful, most would fall to their knees when the call comes. Your first push back is how would you know you will be called? If you are a new human and practice Kriya Serpent Yoga, you will be called.

When I received my purpose through multiple visions over several months (daytime visions while going about my day), it was clear I must wake up the new humans who will be integral to the next millennium of human evolution. We are on the cusp of entering a new age in human existence, and all these new humans are the architects, builders and operators of that new world.

Kriya Serpent Yoga is the method I was given to wake you up and reconnect you to the Divine so you learn your purpose. That is what this book is all about. No religion. No cult. No tithing. No power grab. No dictation of reality to non-believers.

Our purpose is simple. When called upon to act on the behalf of your Creator, accept your purpose and work your remaining years to accomplish it. If you cannot complete it in this lifetime, ensure others can pick up the torch and carry it forward.

If you can't or won't do this, then Kriya Serpent Yoga is not for you. Go find a different yoga where there is no expectation of working for your Creator. It is your life, live it the way you want to, but if you are like me and want to do something in this lifetime that will benefit humanity's future, then please continue.

I am not trying to scare you, tempt you, or persuade you to do anything you do not want to do. I am here only to wake you up, help you understand when you are called to action and hopefully help facilitate your actions so that you can be successful in your purpose.

There is nothing but good things here. You will never be called to harm, hurt, oppress, or kill anyone or anything because that is not what the Divine wants. You may be called upon to change something broken in this world, like pollution, financial instability, social discord, mental illness, fundamental human rights, etc. We are the good guys because we work for the good Guy/Gal/God.

Over the next millennium, humanity will heal, discover incredible revelations, create impossible technologies, achieve spiritual enlightenment and accept spiritual guidance. The Divine will work through us to create a better world for humanity. I am not talking Heaven on earth. That is a religious concept I do not subscribe to. I am talking about a humanity that is in balance with the earth, all the creatures within the Universe and the Divine. It would be more correct to say we are taking earth to Heaven.

Now, I get it, there are plenty of people telling you this is the right religion or the right belief or the right practice if you want to progress in your spiritual evolution. Who do you believe? A school teacher/engineer who supposedly speaks to the Divine? Maybe he is just another in a long line of charlatans trying to fool you into believing some new age tale of unicorns and angels or some such stuff. *I get it!*

To help you out, I will address this doubt. As my former life in the Soka Gakkai International taught me, *the proof is in the* pudding. If you choose to move on, see if you establish a connection to the Divine. Determine if you are called upon for a purpose. If you are not, move on to something else. If you experience nothing, chalk it up to me being a fraud or charlatan.

None of what I am doing is because I came up with it. I didn't. It was all given to me in a series of visions, and then further refined in conversations with the Divine during my meditations. Honestly, before this, I was preparing for a retirement of leisure. It was going to be golf, travel, drinking and eating, while having fun with family and friends.

But then the call came in, and I answered with a resounding yes, so here is the book that is part of my purpose. I have so much more to do, but this is the very first step. I am happy. I have purpose, and yes, I still have fun with family and friends. I simply have less free time than I had imagined. I have no regrets and will pursue this until my final breath. *But can you do that?*

If you think so, then answer the simple question. If you are called, will you answer and accept the purpose you are given? If your answer is yes, then proceed with this level of practice. If you say yes, you will be forever changed in a way you cannot yet fathom. Like the quote at the beginning of this chapter stated, "The better your practice, the brighter your flame." Burn bright and light the way into the next millennium.

Objective Skills

1. **Sit in meditation**: We further develop this skill and extend meditation time. *Mastery* is achieved when you can sit comfortably without moving or discomfort for the entirety of your session.

2. **Counting beads**: This is fundamental to all Kriya Serpent techniques. *Mastery* is using Mala beads to count all repetitions.
3. **Moving Energy through Chakras**: Integrate moving energy through chakras into your Kriya Serpent practice. *Mastery* is attained when you can stimulate each chakra.
4. **Serpent Fire**: A new technique to enhance Kundalini. *Mastery* is when you can intone all the sounds while visualizing the associated symbols.
5. **Bandha**: Stimulate an intense rush of Kundalini using a Bandha. *Mastery* is when you can elicit a final surge of energy before altered states.
6. **Meditating**: New techniques to move you towards your purpose and service to your Creator. Mastery is when you achieve altered states of consciousness, an inner guru, spirit guides and the Creator.

As mentioned in the introduction, you will focus now on discovering your purpose and extending your Kriya Serpent practice. To quote one of the greatest Gurus of all time, Yoda: *No more training do you require. Already know you, that which you need.* This does not mean you are done learning, but you have all the basic skills you need for success at this level.

There are two new techniques at this level. One is just a modification to the *Song of the Serpent* from the previous level. The other technique is a type of bandha I learned through reading SantataGamana's book on Tantric Yoga titled *Tantra Exposed*.

Traditional Techniques

Variation of Tantric Fire

This technique was borrowed from SantataGamana's book titled *Tantra Exposed*. I have changed it for our Kriya Serpent practice because it follows Serpent Fire when the Kundalini is very active. However, this technique is a great way to end your exercises before you meditate.

In my variation of this technique, I will have you think of something specific you love (family, God, etc.). In SantataGamana's variation, he talks about Bliss in the Heart chakra, but for many, bliss may be a very nebulous concept that most cannot yet get their head around.

Instead, I'll have you focus on love for something specific that brings you happiness. I use people in my life and spiritual entities to think about and focus on that feeling of love. If you do the same thing, you will eventually feel the bliss associated with your love.

1. Sit in meditation.
2. Focus on someone you love and direct those feelings into your Heart chakra.
3. Inhale slowly, then hold the breath for 30–60 seconds.
4. During the breath hold, contract your anal sphincter and perineum as though you are preventing your body from going to the bathroom. Lock them fully and hold while you hold your breath.
5. Exhale slowly as you release the sphincter and perineum lock. You will likely feel your Kundalini rise on the exhalation, and if so, channel it through your Crown chakra.
6. Repeat steps 2 through 5 two (2) more times for a total count of three (3).

This may be difficult for some people, even if holding in your waste is something you do naturally. Being asked to do it while meditating is challenging. However, through practice, you find you can hold it for as long as needed.

As soon as I lock those muscles during the breath hold, I feel energy in my extremities, pulling inward towards my Base chakra, activating the Kundalini. On the exhalation, the Kundalini explodes in an intense surge, often more powerful than during Serpent Fire. After three, I am in an elevated and altered state of consciousness to begin meditation.

I believe you will experience something similar and see why it is a great way to end the other techniques prior to meditation. However, it is optional, and if you feel you activated sufficient Kundalini during Serpent Fire, skip this technique.

Kriya Serpent Techniques

Serpent Fire

You should have the symbols and sounds already memorized in their proper order. If not, please refer to the previous chapter for the list of the four symbols. As in the previous techniques, you will chant the sounds while visualizing the symbols. However, unlike Song of the Serpent in Level 2, you will move your energy up and down the spinal channel while intoning each sound, as you did in Pranayama.

This new technique should intensify the Kundalini response to the chanting by stimulating each of the main chakras during the practice. You will still only need 2 breaths for one cycle, and you will intone 2 sounds for each breath as before. Now, however, you will also focus on the energy within your body, bringing it up into your Third Eye chakra from the Base chakra, and then down again on the exhale.

This is like the Pranayama technique in the previous chapter, except now you intone the Kriya Serpent sounds rather than Ohm in each chakra. It is like combining the previous two techniques.

1. Sit in meditation.
2. Count up beads.
3. Inhale and mentally chant "Ah" as you visualize the *Manifest* symbol. While inhaling, focus on bringing your energy, like your breath, up through the spinal column from the Base chakra into your Third Eye chakra (Center brain), as though you are filling your head with energy like a balloon. Pause for 2 counts.
4. Exhale and mentally chant "Ee" as you visualize the *Protect* symbol. While exhaling, focus on moving the energy down the spinal column from your Third Eye chakra to your Base chakra. Pause for 2 counts.
5. Inhale and mentally chant "Ohm" as you visualize the Divine symbol. While inhaling, focus on bringing your energy, like your breath, up the spinal column from the Base chakra into your Third Eye chakra (Center brain), as though you were filling your head with energy like a balloon. Pause for 2 counts.
6. Exhale and mentally chant "Uh" as you visualize the *Rebirth* symbol. While exhaling, focus on moving the energy down the spinal column from your Third Eye chakra to your Base chakra. Pause 2 counts.
7. You have completed 1 cycle of this technique, so count down 1 bead. You should feel a cool sensation along your spine after the energy moves through it, and your focus should be on moving the energy through each chakra from Base to Third Eye and back again. This will stimulate all the main chakras as in Pranayama.
8. Repeat steps 3–7 until you have completed your total count.
9. Your Kundalini should rise, and when it does, direct it into your Crown chakra as in the *Song of the Serpent* technique. This is important. Expect the Kundalini to rise in either of the exhalations, though it will usually be the last one.

The following are the levels you should achieve with this technique. Start slowly and work your way up:

- **Beginner**: 24 cycles,
- **Intermediate**: 36 cycles, and
- **Advanced**: 48 cycles.

You may have noticed I do not advocate counting beyond 60 for any of the Kriya Serpent techniques. Since we are stimulating the Kundalini so often with this practice, many repetitions are not needed. In Kriya Yoga, and others, mastery is typically defined as the full count of 108 beads.

I have done 48 counts of Serpent Fire before, and it was quite intense. The heat generated from this technique can almost bring a sweat, and might for some people. You are moving a lot of energy up and down your spine while raising the Kundalini repeatedly through most, if not all, of the full count. That is a lot of energy, and it will generate a lot of heat, so be prepared. This is why I named it *Serpent Fire*.

I usually do 36 counts in my daily regimen, but there will be some who want more, so 48 should be sufficient. Any more than that, and you might see a manifestation of side effects, some less pleasant. However, if you are fully adapted to the Kundalini, the positive effects will be wonderful.

This is where you connect to the Divine, experiencing deeper states of consciousness while opening your mind to the truth of reality. Many of these experiences were listed on the previous levels, so be prepared for a wonderful, and yet unusual, journey.

In the meditation phase of your daily practice, the Kundalini may periodically rise. Sometimes, it rises with an intensity you're not prepared for. Keep in mind, you stimulated the Kundalini significantly through Serpent Fire, and it is still active even while meditating.

This transforms your session into something interactive rather than the stillness and calm on the previous levels. In my meditation sessions, I am often in deep conversations with the Divine, spirit guides, or Avatars. They instruct me on life, this practice, and my purpose. It is the Kundalini that unlocks the spiritual door through which masters may assist you.

Meditating

I moved the meditating techniques into the Kriya Serpent techniques section, since we are now focused on finding your purpose and guides who will help you. These techniques assist you in creating the proper environment for these guides to come through. Kundalini opens the door, but your will and focus help you and others walk through it.

The first technique begins the separation of your Soul (ethereal) from your ego (material). Interactions between the two make up how you view yourself. But you only realize half of these two parts. We are eternal Souls, and this body and ego are manifestations of that Soul on the material plane. Your ego is not you, just you in this incarnation created by your experiences and conditioning.

Our goal is to separate the two as independent entities so you realize the true you. This is the basic premise of Buddhism, quelling the ego so the Soul emerges. Once it does, amazing things manifest in your life.

You will develop compassion, communicate across the Cosmos through a Universal Ocean of consciousness, relive memories of past lives, and establish a connection to the Divine within. Essentially, you are separating your *consciousness* from your *material senses*.

However, we stop short of full realization because we are an integral part of this material reality in the service of our Creator. Our senses are important on the material plane, so we will not let them go entirely. Instead, we awaken our Soul, which guides our ego as we pursue our purpose. We are not searching for Nirvana. We are searching for our true self and its purpose in this lifetime.

Visualization #1

1. Sit in meditation.
2. Meditate in the stillness of a gray sphere for 5 minutes as you sink into deeper states of consciousness.
3. Focus on the point between your eyes for a count of 10.
4. Through visualization, shift your focus outside yourself, looking at you meditating on the point between your eyes. Bring this visualization to life as you see yourself sitting in meditation. Look at the details of your face.
5. Now, turn your focus to the room around you. Starting directly behind your meditating form, scan the room and identify every piece of furniture, objects, colors and textures as you float above your meditating form.
6. Now shift your focus back to your meditating form sitting and rotate around yourself noticing every aspect of your body. Notice your skin, your face, your hair, your clothing, how you are sitting and how you are breathing.
7. This is the incarnation of you, and it contains the ego. If you are your ego, you would not be floating above your body looking down on it. Your consciousness is a separate entity from the form you are looking at. When you have clarified the view of yourself sufficiently, pull yourself back into your body and focus on the point between your eyes once more.
8. Feel the sensations of your body as it sits in silence. What do you smell? What do you feel? What sensations do you feel through your body at this very moment? Focus on those sensations. These are your senses, and your senses

are part of your *material* self. Did you feel these sensations the same way when you were floating above yourself?

While this exercise may seem a bit silly, it is an important part of your transformation into your consciousness. Your consciousness is free to travel anywhere in the Universe while your body and ego must stay sitting in meditation.

When I first began this exercise, I found it difficult to visualize the room and all the objects within it. This harkens back to the visualization techniques outlined in earlier chapters. If need be, go back and review those practices to help you with this exercise.

The next visualization technique comes from several sources but will connect you with your Soul and let it fly free of your material body.

Visualization #2

1. Sit in meditation.
2. Meditate in the stillness of a gray sphere for 5 minutes as you sink into deeper states of consciousness.
3. Focus your inner sight on the point between your eyes for a count of 10.
4. Shift your focus to the back of the inside of your head and see your eyes on the other side of the inside of your head.
5. Shift your focus to the left side of your head and see how the view of your eyes shifted.
6. Shift your focus on the right side of your head and see how the view of your eyes shifted once again.
7. Shift your focus outside your head looking down at your seated form. Slowly move that focus up to the ceiling so you see the entirety of the room and its objects.
8. Now shift your focus outside the building where your room is and see it from a high vantage point.

9. Continue shifting your view as though something is pulling you upward into the sky. Stop when you see the entirety of earth floating in the blackness of space. Look at the details of the land versus water. See how the clouds form a soft blanket across the planet.
10. Now shift your view to the distant moon. Shift your focus instantly so you are standing on the moon looking back at earth.
11. Shift your focus to the moonscape around you. Bend down and pick up lunar dirt and feel it as it spills from your hand.
12. Using your imagination, leave the moon going away from the sun as though you are being pulled by an invisible force. Visualize passing Mars, the asteroid belt, Jupiter, Saturn, Uranus and Neptune. Stop and look back at the sun. See how small it is against a backdrop of blackness illuminated by billions of stars.
13. Shifting your focus, return the way you came, passing each planet before stopping at the moon. Then stop above earth before moving down to your body once more.

This is a great exercise to remind us how insignificant we are compared to the grandeur of the Cosmos. The truth is we are not insignificant to our Creator. We may be a mote in the body of our Creator, but we are part of the Creator and the Creator is part of us. This makes us important, and that is why we have a role to play in this incarnation.

One might question, is this really me traveling, or is it just me making things up in my head? A deep question, but one I cannot answer without giving you a question in return. Follow my chain of thought.

We are all energy in a great ocean of energy we call the Universe. Thought is energy emanating from our brains. Consciousness is our Soul energy manifesting our mind and body in this material plane, which are just energy. So when you ask if this exercise is real or your imagination, you are actually asking *is this energy really energy,* and the answer is yes.

As you pull your focus (consciousness) away from your body and ego, you free it to travel anywhere within the Ocean of consciousness we live within. Everything we see with our senses is nothing but energy controlled by consciousness. Ergo, your imagination is your consciousness, which is free to traverse anywhere there is Universal consciousness.

This is also the basis for manifesting in the material plane that which we desire. We imagine it, thus creating it in the ethereal plane, and if it is not opposed by the Divine or natural laws, it will be made manifest in the material plane. In Buddhism, we are taught we are the ones who make the reality we experience. What we think drives what we are. So the question to you is: is there a difference between what you imagine and what is real?

This may not sit well right now, but as you separate from your ego and discover more about the reality you cannot yet perceive, you will understand what I am talking about. For now, focus on making your visualizations or imaginations as real as possible. Eventually, you will understand there is no difference between what you assume is real and what you imagine is real.

This exercise can be extended to traveling outside our solar system into other solar systems or galaxies. As part of my mystical practice, I travel to a place outside our galaxy, where I have met other mystics from whom I have learned much. At this stage, I never wonder if such a place is real or only in my mind because either way, it is real.

At least once, have fun with this exercise and try the following activity. I have done this many times. Focus on finding the International Space Station (ISS), and then visualize yourself sitting on top of it, riding it around the earth. Mind blowing, fun, and a great way to realize there are multiple planes of existence all around us.

The Inner Guru

This next exercise within our meditation is all about contacting your inner guru. As I have stated before, your inner guru is a connection to the Divine part of you called your Soul. Your inner guru is wise, as it has access to all your past lives and experiences. It is also a part of the Creator, therefore, it taps into Divine wisdom.

So how does one contact this inner guru? While I can't speak for others, mine started talking to me in one of my meditations. In fact, I believe I was contemplating my first Kundalini experience, trying to figure out what had happened that first time. Keep in mind, I knew nothing about Samadhi when I experienced Kundalini.

In my mind, a soft voice spoke out and told me I had experienced the disintegration of my ego and the union of my Soul with Source or Creator. I didn't know if this was the inner guru I had heard about, so I asked. It confirmed it was.

Now, if you tell people you are hearing voices in your head, you might get taken away in a straightjacket, so let's be clear about what is happening here. You have developed your focus, meditated and entered altered states of consciousness, raised your vibrational energy through Kundalini and ascended into different planes of reality.

Okay, for some, that already sounds crazy, but it is very real and the reason you began this practice. You wanted to see the "real" reality, not just what your ego tells you is real. You wanted to re-connect with the Divine within you, find your purpose and have the Divine guide you to complete that purpose. This is Kriya Serpent Yoga, so not crazy, but a solemn practice for the betterment of yourself and humanity.

I will agree it is not for everybody. This is designed for new humans ready to grab the reins of our material existence to lead us into the enlightened world of the next millennium.

If you are here, you are likely one of those new humans. If so, let's search within to find your inner guru.

1. Sit in meditation.
2. Meditate in the stillness of a gray sphere for 5 minutes as you sink into deeper states of consciousness.
3. Focus inward on the point between your eyes for a count of 10.
4. Think of a metaphysical question you have been pondering for some time. Perhaps it is something like, *have I been reincarnated in this lifetime?* After all, I didn't believe at first.
5. Now, offer your gratitude to the Creator for all the things in your life and ask your question.
6. Wait in stillness and observe whatever sounds, lights, or images come to you.
7. After a few minutes, whether you receive an answer or not, give your thanks for listening to your request. If you receive an answer, you may attempt a conversation with the voice, but always be grateful and thankful for their advice.

Keep trying and do not be discouraged if it doesn't happen immediately. Think of it this way. When you are ready for that conversation to take place (something only they would know), then it will happen. It isn't that you're unworthy; it is because you are not ready, so keep practicing.

Once you hold *many* conversations with your inner guru, do this exercise once more, but ask what your *purpose* is. Just like that initial communication, finding your purpose is all about being ready for it. They will know and might even reveal you are not ready when you ask.

I never even thought to ask, because that was not why I was practicing yoga. It was not part of my teachings, so I never even thought to ask if I had a purpose. For me, it was thrust upon me while driving through the deserts of Arizona coming back from a vacation.

You might experience the same thing, or not. Everyone's experience may be different, but do not shy away from it once you have established communication with your inner guru. I want to make one last comment about your inner guru. There is communication with your Soul and there is intuition. I posit they are the same thing as I believe our intuition comes from our Soul as does our inner guru. Intuition disguises itself as our own thoughts and feelings, but those thoughts and feelings are but the interactions of our Soul with our minds.

Our inner guru is like our personal Master, and it will guide us, teach us and help us with our lives and practice. Through your inner guru, you will learn about past lives, understand your karma and learn how to achieve your purpose. Honest gratitude and humility are the keys to this relationship that will serve you throughout the rest of this lifetime and beyond.

Daily Regimen

Just like the earlier chapters, we split this level into two different phases. Overall, this level should take only 3–6 months for most practitioners. Serpent Fire is a fabulous technique which raises your Kundalini readily, allowing you to progress rapidly in your spiritual evolution and practice.

Phase 1: Isolating the Ego (1–3 months)

Our goal is to create the separation between your consciousness and your ego. Using the visualization techniques, you will start that separation process immediately, beginning to see yourself as something other than what your ego says you are.

Our goal is to connect you with your inner guru and find your purpose, but separation is a requisite step. Once you see yourself as more than your ego, you will stir the Soul to action thus bringing forth your inner guru. Be patient and focus for significant results.

Beginner Level Daily Regimen (40 minutes total):

1. Sitting in Meditation: Duration of session,
2. Nadi Shodhana: 6 counts,
3. Ujjayi Breathing: 6 counts,
4. Serpent Fire: 24 cycles,
5. Tantric Fire Variation: 3 counts, and
6. Meditating: 15 minutes.

Intermediate Level Daily Regimen (45 minutes total):

1. Sitting in Meditation: Duration of session,
2. Nadi Shodhana: 6 counts,
3. Ujjayi Breathing: 12 counts,
4. Serpent Fire: 36 cycles,
5. Tantric Fire Variation: 3 counts, and
6. Meditating: 20 minutes.

Advanced Level Daily Regimen (60 minutes total):

1. Sitting in Meditation: Duration of session,
2. Nadi Shodhana: 6 counts,
3. Ujjayi Breathing: 12 counts,
4. Serpent Fire: 48 cycles,
5. Tantric Fire Variation: 3 counts, and
6. Meditating: 30 minutes.

While meditating, complete one of the *two visualization* techniques, alternating each day between the two. Over time, you may enjoy one more than the other. This is okay, but it is important to see yourself meditating from different points of view to get the full benefit. Don't neglect this aspect of the techniques.

Once you are regularly practicing the advanced level of this daily regimen, you may move on to Phase 2.

Phase 2: Inner Guru (1–3 months)

At this stage in your training, we no longer need to have differing levels of practice. Early on when you were learning new techniques, it was important for you to start slower. Now, you should have a regular 60–90-minute practice every day.

<u>Daily Regimen (60–90 minutes total):</u>

1. Sitting in Meditation: Duration of session,
2. Nadi Shodhana: 6 counts,
3. Ujjayi Breathing: 12 counts,
4. Serpent Fire: 36–48 cycles.
5. Tantric Fire Variation: 3 counts, and
6. Meditating: 30–40 minutes.

It is possible you might want to practice Serpent Fire for a count of 48, and that is certainly an option. You can even extend your meditation period further if you have the time. However, those are personal choices you must make based on your experiences and what those experiences are telling you.

The regimen I outlined was my daily routine for a long while. It generates sufficient Kundalini while yielding benefits of the altered states of consciousness. I held many conversations with Celestial entities including my inner guru, and grew remarkably fast in my spiritual practice through this regimen.

While you meditate, use the *inner guru technique* to start this phase of your journey. Begin with simple questions and wait until you have established communication before pressing for your purpose. It will come with time.

As mentioned earlier, it is important to understand your purpose will be given to you at a time when you are most able to commit and execute. That may not be now. Instead, you may be directed to broaden your spiritual knowledge to prepare for that next stage in your evolution.

The key is to deepen your practice, contact your inner guru and follow their lead on how to proceed forward. This could be your daily practice for a long time, so relish the benefits you will receive from it. Do not despair if your purpose has not yet been revealed.

However, once your purpose is revealed, move on to the next level. While I stated this level is 3–6 months in duration, it may be years for some people. It depends so much on your prior lives, your prior spiritual growth and your innate wisdom accumulated in this life and all others. You will grow if this is all you do for the rest of your life. This is powerful stuff, and you will evolve if you maintain this daily regimen.

The next chapter contains variations on the existing techniques intended to help you achieve your purpose through assistance from the Divine. I am talking about downloads of information and ideas you can implement immediately to apply to your purpose.

Warnings, Suggestions and Side Effects

Everything listed in the prior chapters applies here, but at this stage, you shouldn't experience the negative aspects related to Kundalini. However, there are a few areas I want to touch upon since you have progressed to this point.

Inner Guru

Contacting your inner guru is significant, and it is important you cultivate a healthy relationship. First, understand that spiritual growth only comes from doing the work. That encompasses all aspects of your practice and life. While it is easy to use your inner guru as some sort of informational repository or leader figure, it is you who must decide, do the work and find what you need to accomplish your goals.

Your inner guru provides the inspiration, knowledge of your past lives, ideas you can use, but you use that information to progress forward. Let me give you an example.

Let's say your inner guru shows you a vision of a past life where you spent most of that life as a peasant toiling in the fields for others only to die young, having accomplished nothing. It is tempting to question your inner guru on why this life is the one being shown to you. How does this apply to my life now? How does it apply to my purpose? How can I use this information to evolve and grow? You get the idea.

All of those questions are *your* work to do, not your inner guru's work. Every past life I have been shown has been something I needed to know for my current incarnation. However, I didn't realize it until I spent a lot of time thinking about it, meditating on it and dissecting it to understand what lessons I could unravel from that snippet of my past. This is your spiritual journey, and if you do not do the hard work, you will not evolve but stagnate.

My inner guru has given me past lives, inspiring ideas and even warnings, but I do not grill him with questions I can answer if I think about them earnestly. That is the spiritual work you must do. It is the proverbial, "you can lead a horse to water but you cannot make him drink." Your inner guru will bring you to the water, but you must drink for yourself. It is you who must awaken.

Celestial Entities

Okay, no unicorns here, but you need to know that the Universe is teeming with life. There are countless entities on many spiritual planes, and you have now been given a ticket to access some of those planes. Taking cues from Dr. Greer, you are an ambassador for humanity and should conduct yourself appropriately. *I am being quite serious.*

I have contacted multiple entities, some in our third dimension and some in higher dimensions. With few exceptions, I was greeted with love and concern. I am very grateful for these opportunities and always show humility. Many are more evolved lifeforms, both physically and spiritually, and this puts us in a subordinate position when interacting with them.

I recommended in the last chapter you should consider simply telling them you are not ready for conversations, and for many of them, they will know this before you say it. This is dangerous territory for any human to tread because we are still trying to come to terms with the fact that we are not alone.

While I have always known there were life forms out there, I didn't know what those forms might be or how I might contact them over such extreme distances. Well, it turns out that distance isn't the barrier we once thought. However, there are humans here on earth who do not want us to reach out to other entities and make contact. The idea of an ordinary citizen contacting other worldly beings without guidance and protocol makes them very uneasy to downright concerned.

Remember, we do not intend to cause friction between ourselves and the current Homo sapiens running this world. Their time is ending and we need only wait for that to happen. So anything you do here may have ramifications with regard to the old guard. Do not stir up trouble because that will get you distracted from your purpose of helping humanity evolve.

Do not be fooled, many of our leaders know of these Celestial entities and even how an average citizen may contact them, but they don't want everyone doing it. So my advice to you starting out is DO NOT reach out to these entities until you are more spiritually evolved. That may take years for many. There will come a time in this life when you are ready, but right now may not be that time.

All the beings I have been in contact with know everything about humanity and our evolution. Many are waiting patiently for this new age to come about so that they can finally make full contact and help us with our evolution. They are ready to assist, but many have been told not to interfere with us just yet. *And rightfully so!* Do you think most people are ready for such a revelation? We will get there eventually.

Humanity's ascension into the Cosmos will happen once we complete specific milestones. Your awakening through this practice is one of those milestones we must all achieve. You are taking a big step into a more expansive Universe than you imagined, and playing on that field is a whole new ball game.

Have proper humility and put all hubris aside. We are children awakening to the knowledge that there are adults on the playground, who will treat us as children until we prove otherwise. I liken it to a toddler walking into a lecture on thermodynamics.

None of this is meant to scare you. Honestly, you may never be contacted by any entities. However, for some of you, this contact will be a requisite part of your purpose because you will need to learn critical knowledge from them. If they contact you, it is because they believe you are ready for that contact. But you still have free will and can tell them no. This is where your inner guru can guide you.

Keep in mind, all of these entities are creations of the one Creator, and therefore are part of the loving family we call our Universe. Do not fear them, for they look forward to the day when we can join them. However, like children, we have much to learn before we can graduate into their Universe.

Now, I don't want to get biblical or anything, but you need to understand something. Not all entities have humanity's best interests at heart. When a young and ignorant species suddenly develops nuclear weapons and sets them off randomly without warning, it causes distress within the Cosmos. Remember, everything is energy and nuclear weapons are tremendous energy.

Now, I am not an expert on these things, but I imagine the ripples from such an explosion are felt not only across the three-dimensional Universe, but across other dimensions. Their impact on those dimensions is unknown, but common sense would dictate it may not be a good thing.

I want to keep this simple and say, there are some entities out there who are not on team humanity. Remember, everyone in the Universe has free will, and that means some may choose not to accept those less evolved than themselves. Tell me you cannot think of humans who do not accept certain species they consider less evolved. Enough said.

There is so much more to this topic, but I will wait and publish another book that will take this on. Just be aware that your practice will awaken you to them and they will see you. Because of that, an interaction is possible though not guaranteed. Caution is warranted, and the best course is to decline politely until you feel ready to engage.

As a cautionary tale, I will recount a prior experience when I was naïve and just starting down this path. I had used Dr. Greer's CE-5 Protocol to expand my consciousness out into our solar system, attempting to locate spacecraft. After locating one, I shifted my focus onto the ship. The method I employed is known as *Astral Projection*.

I was not very good at it, and everything within the ship shimmered with static. There was an entity sitting at the controls of the ship in front of me. I watched silently until a voice spoke in my head, telling me to get out. I sensed anger, so I left.

A couple of days later, I was driving my car home from the market. As I passed through a large intersection into my neighborhood, I saw a bright flash of white light out of the corner of my left eye as something slammed into my car, making it rock back and forth, nearly causing me to swerve off the road.

At first, I thought I had hit some bicyclist who had slammed into me. But as I checked my mirrors, there was nothing behind me. I was shaken. What had hit me so hard? The sound and force was like that of a human body slamming into the rear side of my vehicle. The car behind me must have seen nothing because it kept driving on as normal, no flashing lights or anything. I was stunned and recounted this incident to several people afterwards.

Given time to think about this incident, I came to what I believe was the correct conclusion. I believe the entity whose ship I had projected onto was giving me an experience similar to what I had given him. The force of my consciousness traveling into his ship may have been like his traveling into mine (car).

I know this sounds ridiculous, but I am convinced I was being given a lesson on proper etiquette for Astral Projection. How would you feel if some alien just appeared in your car while you were driving? Now, I wasn't hurt by the incident, but it taught me a valuable lesson. This is genuine power, and we must use it with humility, wisdom and practice, or we may make terrible mistakes.

In a future book, I will reveal more about this entity and my early interactions with them leading up to a pivotal life event for both of us. We apparently had a long-term relationship only he had been aware of. But that is for another book. I learned my lesson and now treat all Astral Projections with humility and care.

If you want more information on this, please refer to my *Resources* chapter at the end of the book.

Spirit Guides and Avatars

If this spooks you, I apologize since that is not my intention. Kriya Serpent Yoga helps us evolve both physically and spiritually so we attain enlightenment, wisdom, knowledge and connect to our Soul with gifts for the betterment of all.

You should not be surprised the Universe is filled with diverse life. Spirit Guides, or what I call Avatars, are just another part of that diversity. They are spirits here to assist us, and often take on the Avatar of someone we know. For example, my first spirit guide was in the Avatar of Gandhi. It was quite wonderful.

You may or may not meet these spirit guides during meditation. So, who are they? While I don't have a definitive answer, I do have theories. I believe these spirits are the enlightened spirits of those who have evolved beyond the physical plane. They take on Avatars to help us connect with them, and in reality, they likely have no corporeal form at all. They are pure energy or spirit from higher dimensions.

This is purely my speculation, but some things Paramahansa Yogananda said in his autobiography led me to believe my speculation may be true. I'll let you read his book and judge for yourself. I have read little literature on this topic, since it is not been something I have sought. For now, I am grateful for my spirit guides and learn as much as I can from them.

I like to think of them as bodhisattvas of the spiritual realm. They want to help us evolve. Now, I have had a recent experience during the writing of this book that has given me the idea that some of them may be past gurus or masters guiding us from beyond the veil. In either case, we can acquire a lot of wisdom from them.

I first met mine in a lucid dream, and it is likely you will too. Mine instructed me to seek him out anytime I have a lucid dream. I do that, and he teaches me things about meditation during lucid dreams and while in my regular meditation.

You are probably wondering why only in lucid dreams. I have given this a lot of thought, and I believe that if they are beyond the veil, this may be the only way to reach them. I mean, we may see images of them in meditation, but no communication. This way, we can see them, interact with them and learn from them.

Lucid dreams are a very special altered state of perception that is different from regular meditation.

I have more experiences and advice from other people about this topic, which leads me to believe that contacting beyond the veil is truly possible and a genuine gift. I know there are those psychics who say they can talk to those who have left this plane of existence, but I have no experience with those people. I haven't even met one, but I must say I tend to believe it is possible.

Whenever you meet one of these spirit guides treat them as you would a guru or any other master. They will instruct you and help you grow spiritually. Learn from their wisdom.

Judeo-Christian Theology

Because you are crossing into a more expansive Universe, you may wonder how this fits into your Judeo-Christian background. You are correct in asking such questions, and it is reasonable I should provide some context around these topics in relation to that background.

Paramahansa Yogananda's autobiography spoke of the spiritually uplifting aspects of his practice. He believed in a single unifying entity or God, and he was a fan of Jesus. I am also a fan of Jesus. However, the great Yogi shied away from the negative aspects of Judeo-Christian theology because his belief that what you think is what you experience kept his mind far from the negative aspects of theology.

I am not here to teach you such theology, nor offer you an alternative to it. But I must allay your fears when I talk about Celestial entities. There are negative energies within the Universe, and it is quite possible you may encounter them. I have encountered such entities at an earlier age in my life, and it transformed me.

So let me address this. If you seek or welcome negative energies into your life, they will gladly come, wreaking havoc and causing chaos. It is what they do. Think of them as the antithesis of all the positive things in the Universe. They are not three-dimensional entities, are typically smarter and more powerful than you. It is unwise to seek them out.

However, if any take an interest in you, it is probably because your ego does not believe in a guiding Universal presence helping us evolve. They will be attracted to you because you can be manipulated because of your lack of a genuine connection to the Divine. These energies will promise much and take even more. Their goal is to turn you into an agent of chaos. They feed off your energy and the energy of the chaos you create.

Follow the Kriya Serpent Yoga practice, and you will be protected from such entities. Your Creator truly loves you and only wants positive outcomes for your spirit, your life and your happiness. The negative energies do not want that for you.

Whenever I have a Celestial visitor, they must confirm two things. One, they must verify they are in the service of our Creator, and two, they must show they come in love? The love must be shown physically, and after you experience the love of your Creator, it cannot be faked. In Kriya Yoga, they call it *Bliss*.

I don't want any of this for you, and more than likely you will never have this problem because you will do what I instruct you to. Simply exercise your free will and send them on their way. Later, as you mature and learn more about our complex and diverse Universe, you will be better able to discern whether an entity is positive or negative.

I realize these topics often cause concern, but if you are practicing as I outline, then you are connected with the Divine within. Realize you have nothing but great prosperity ahead of you. Banish the fear of the unknown, and understand you are a powerful and positive force for our Creator, helping humanity into the next millennium.

Once you are truly awake, you will no longer fear anything in the Universe because your Creator's love will protect you and nourish you. There is nothing more powerful out there. You will not fear death because you know you will reincarnate again to carry on with your work. You will be an unstoppable force as you pursue your purpose with the full support of the Universe backing you.

The Next Level

You should move onto the next level once you have discovered your purpose. At that stage, it is all about continuing your spiritual development and growth, while pursuing your purpose. If you have not yet found your purpose, do not despair. Continue your practice at this level and you will grow, eventually finding your purpose.

Some warnings I mentioned earlier may give pause, and rightfully so. But as an engineer, I have always believed that you cannot fully complete the task at hand without knowledge of the potential pitfalls you may encounter. While I can't detail all the pitfalls, I have attempted to outline some and give you wise guidance on how to deal with them.

However, if you are still uneasy, then you may not have the maturity either spiritually or physically to handle this yet. That is okay. It is not a race, but a journey spanning many lifetimes. If you are uneasy, please stop, go try other things and see what fits you best.

As an Indigo Child with paranormal experience, I am better equipped to navigate this precarious Universe of diversity and alternate planes of existence. I recognize the Universe has a balance to it, which many refer to as Yin and Yang. Some call it positive and negative, while others say masculine and feminine.

Opposite polarities are inherent within our reality. If you choose to become a mystic, you will understand these polarities better. If not, don't worry, because there is a bountiful life of experience and knowledge you can still explore without Kriya Serpent Yoga.

Knowing people as I do over my lifetimes, I can often tell who is prepared for such a diverse Universe and who is not. If you believe you are not, have no shame and move on to something that better resonates with you.

For those of you who want an opportunity to play a role in this complex Universe, then Kriya Serpent Yoga is your path. Move on to the next level and work on your purpose, joining the millions of new humans who will work beside you.

Chapter 9

Meditation is not a way of making your mind quiet. It's a way of entering into the quiet that's already there.
Deepak Chopra

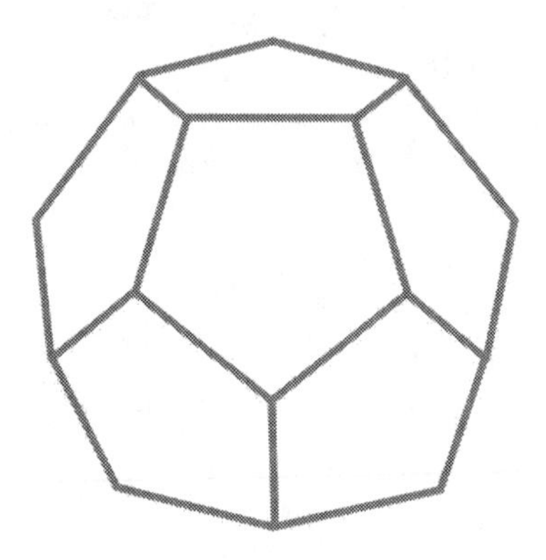

Advanced Level 4

Introduction

I honestly don't know who could not love Deepak Chopra. He is a man who knows his purpose and is helping people all over the world. Yes, the quiet is already there. To borrow from Matias De Stefano, "I am" is that quiet within us all.

To know your origins, your Creator, and your true self is "I am," and once you have, you can never turn away from your purpose. That is *why you are here,* to pursue your purpose and find the "I am" within.

At this stage, you have progressed through all the prior levels of Kriya Serpent Yoga and activated your Kundalini as part of your daily regimen. You have entered altered states of consciousness, formed a relationship with your inner guru and found your purpose for this incarnation. Rejoice in your accomplishments. You have taken a solemn oath to serve your Creator by helping humanity into the next stage of our evolution.

This is a fantastic era in human evolution and is like the emergence of a caterpillar from its cocoon. We will take on the ultimate form of a beautiful butterfly, though it will take thousands of years. An emergence is beginning, and you have a front-row seat to this incredible time in history.

Even better, you are an integral part of what will help that emergence. You will bring order to the chaos, love to despair and happiness to the sadness that has gripped humanity for so long. We are not born of sin, but of Divinity. Within all of us is a part of our Creator, and as that part awakens within this reality, the world will emerge from a long slumber into the daylight of truth.

I know this is very poetic and maybe a little sappy, but I mean it. This is the beginning of a very long age of new humans, where ignorance and suffering will end. Our isolation from the rest of the Universe will cease, and our connection with the Divine will finally be re-established. And you have a role in this great revelation.

Your purpose, no matter how small it may seem, is an important part of that overall whole. My purpose is to awaken you, and facilitate the building of the blueprint of humanity for the next millennium. You and all the others who have awakened will be the architects of that blueprint. A new age of humanity will be designed and built rather than organically grown through strife and chaos.

We will all have the backing of the Divine to guide us, providing us with the tools, knowledge and resources we need to make this happen. You will learn to manifest that which you desire, using it to create the end product of your purpose. You will develop new skills and technologies to assist us with this new blueprint. In essence, you will heal and rebuild this world.

Don't be fooled, millions are working on this already. All the practitioners of Kriya Serpent Yoga will join them to play our part in this transformation. Today, we see a world on the brink of collapse. Between global climate change, social evolution and technological progress exceeding science fiction, we are on the brink of an implosion.

Our species is too immature to handle such global events without unseen consequences. We lack foresight, knowledge, wisdom and guidance for such an undertaking. But Kriya Serpent Yoga with other spiritual awakenings will bring maturity to tackle these global problems. We will finally design the world we all deserve.

Your purpose in this lifetime is to promote Kriya Serpent Yoga to awaken others, and to help build this new world. We will begin small, but like the acorn, we will grow into a mighty oak backed by the Divine within us all. We will all be a leaf, branch, or root for this mighty oak, and it shall not perish from this earth, but will stand the test of time as humanity finally fulfills its purpose within the Cosmos.

We will run into obstacles throughout this transformation, but we will not stop. As one falls, another will take their place. You will spend many lifetimes over the next millennium working on this grand transformation, and I can't speak for anyone else, but that makes me very excited.

While I was in engineering, we always ran into obstacles. Sometimes it was money, sometimes it was poor planning and sometimes it was poor design. You don't give up but find a workaround or start again. You never give up. Keep that in mind as you begin your life's purpose and run into obstacles. I have already run into obstacles in pursuit of my purpose, but I have forged onward, adjusting as needed to make continuous progress.

Be in this for the long haul, not just for the next few years. You will spend decades trying to achieve your purpose and may still come up short, but that is okay. As they like to say, Rome wasn't built in a day, and rebuilding this world is the same. Progress will be made in fits and starts until the final product is completed.

If you are ready, proceed into your future.

Objective Skills

We are talking about some rather different things in this level. If you are to advance in your spiritual practice while you pursue your purpose, then you will need education. While each of your paths will be different depending on your spiritual desires and purpose, I can give you general guidance on what you should expect to do.

Yes, we have some new Kriya Serpent techniques that you will learn, but they should help you spiritually with your purpose. I want you to be clear here. If you received your purpose, then it is time to work on it. However, remember what I was told, we don't want to do it fast, but do it *right*.

The following are the objective skills we want to accomplish in this advanced level of Kriya Serpent Yoga.

1. **Serpent Fire**: You will modify this in your new practice. *Mastery* is achieved when you intone sounds while visualizing symbols.
2. **Serpent Star**: A new technique which energizes you. *Mastery* is achieved when you feel the light of your energy in everyday life.
3. **Crystal Serpent**: Eliminate negative energy from your chakras. *Mastery* is when you achieve clarity.
4. **Meditating**: Self-guided sessions to extend your knowledge, increase communication and inspire your purpose. *Mastery* is attained when you obtain data downloads, ideas, knowledge, guidance and wisdom.

5. **Education**: Educating yourself spiritually and on all things related to your purpose. *Mastery* is when you are an expert on your purpose and all things related to it.
6. **Positive Life State**: Improved health, lifestyle and habits. *Mastery* is when you have achieved increased health, vitality, psychology, psychic powers and happiness.
7. **Manifesting**: Creating in this world that which you desire. *Mastery* is when you can bring the new world to life.
8. **Your Purpose**: Steady progress on your purpose. *Mastery* is when your purpose is completed or ready to handoff upon your release from this incarnation.
9. **Kriya Serpent**: Promote and extend Kriya Serpent Yoga as you grow spiritually and gain more wisdom. *Mastery* is *never* achieved as this persists throughout all lifetimes.
10. **Journaling**: Writing about your spiritual growth, conversations and experiences. *Mastery* is once you are creating daily or weekly logs of all significant events in your spiritual practice.

You may have noticed this is the rest of your life and all lives beyond that. You have heard of wash, rinse and repeat? Well incarnate, achieve purpose, reincarnate. In each subsequent incarnation, you will learn more about your prior lives and purposes in each. You will continue to build on that as you grow into the human you were destined to be. The human you were meant to become.

Let's unpack each of these objective skills you will use for the rest of your life.

Serpent Fire

There is nothing new here, but continue the practice to expand your spiritual growth and purpose. The Kundalini is the energy driving you to new horizons and milestones along your journey. However, there is one slight modification.

On this level, channel the Kundalini through the point between your eyes (Bhrumadhya). This will stimulate the Ajna or Third Eye chakra and the frontal lobes of your brain. You will feel genuine changes within your psychological state of mind and will probably experience an uptick in your Siddhis or psychic abilities.

These abilities are gifts from your Creator, who has given you all the tools you need to flower into the new human you are. Embrace these gifts and use them for the betterment of humanity and your own spiritual growth.

Serpent Star

This new technique is all about energizing your Kundalini without the rush and release of it through a chakra. The intent is to build up the energy within your body, and let it resonate within you throughout the day. It will forever change you, but as you might imagine, this is an advanced technique. You will probably feel a state of bliss afterwards.

I said before that when the Kundalini rises, do not stop it as that may cause injury and blockages. This is still true, so if it rises, let it rise. You will advance to a point where you feel the energy activate, but not rise. At that stage, you are ready for Serpent Star.

This is intense enough that it should only be done once a week at most. I typically practice mine on Wednesdays, but your body will find your special day. This activation without rising will happen as you practice Serpent Fire. One day, you will do Serpent Fire as always, but on inhalations and exhalations, no Kundalini will rise. If you notice this, don't force it, but recognize it as a day you can practice Serpent Star.

This will be your cue that you are ready for this advanced technique. I can tell you from experience, the first time is both amazing and filled with anxiety. You will feel energized in a way you haven't before, and it changes your outlook on all things throughout your day. It is very powerful.

Crystal Serpent

This may be at odds with many practitioners of yoga, and I do not hold that against them. But hear me out for a minute. We are all energy. Everything we see and experience is energy. Crystals are conductors of energy. Their lattice and compositional structure are integral to how they conduct energy.

So, if we are all energy, as is everything we know, then it makes sense that conductors of energy are going to impact us and our surroundings. Keep in mind, before this practice, I had never been into crystals or known anyone who was except my wife, and her interest was mild at best.

I come to this from a Kriya Yoga perspective because once I started to energize and attune my body to the subtle energies of the Universe, I sensed and felt the energies of crystals. I believe I recounted earlier about the intense energy that overwhelmed me the first time I took my daughters to the crystal shop. It is real, and it can be intense.

Okay, so what is clearing with crystals all about? Those in the "crystal" know understand that we swim in an ocean of energies. Some of those energies are positive, some are neutral and some are negative. As you become more energetic through this practice, you will interact even more with this ocean of energy, and some of the negative energy collects in your chakras.

Clearing is exactly as it sounds. You will learn how to clear the negative energy that accumulates within your main chakras. It is a simple process, and when it is complete, you will feel the difference. I told my daughter it was like the feeling after eating a mint to cleanse your pallet, except you're cleansing the whole body.

While this is certainly optional, I highly recommend you try it before you discard it. Negative energies will slow your spiritual progress if you never clear them. Think about it, everything gets dirty over time, so do chakras. Clean them weekly, and they will serve you well.

There are certainly other ways of clearing, but I find this technique incredibly easy and refreshing. You will only need two quartz crystals to do this technique. If you cannot find a crystal shop near you, then search online, as I have purchased crystals online successfully.

I suggest each quartz crystal be clear as glass, highly polished and have one end that comes to a point. On Amazon, they call them *Healing Stone Wand of Clear Quartz Crystal Pointed & Faceted Prism Bar*. Okay, before you rush off to Amazon, let me tell you the advantage of buying them in person.

At a crystal shop, you can talk with a knowledgeable crystal person who can help you find what you need. Once you find them, take two of them and hold them in each of your hands with elbows bent at 90 degrees. Place the flat bottom end of the bar perpendicular to your palm with the pointed end sticking up out of your closed fist. Place the center of your thumb print on the pointed end.

Now sense the feeling of these two crystals. Do they feel good? Do you feel the energy flowing out and into your body from them? For me, the two form a circuit that when both thumbs are closed on it, I feel the energy flowing between the two crystals through my body. This is what you want.

If you feel nothing or something negative, move on to other ones. Unfortunately, fake ones abound, so be sure who you are getting them from. Go online and do research to find an excellent source. If any metaphysical fairs come to town, see what they are offering. They will probably have experts who can direct you to somewhere reputable, even if they do not have the crystals you need.

Clearing is a common method to clear negative energy from nearly anything, and I use crystals for more than just my chakras. I also use a crystal to assist with my meditation. I have also placed a large amethyst on my altar. You do not need to do this, but if you are interested in upping your energy, talk with a crystal specialist to see what might work best for you.

The crystal shop I use in Colorado has very knowledgeable personnel and is quite reputable. I have been very satisfied with the crystals I have purchased there. There is also a great crystal shop in Sedona, Arizona, where I purchased the one I hold in my hand during my daily practice. *Incredible!* I have listed some resources in the last chapter of the book to get you started.

Meditating

I will no longer provide you guidance with meditating since you are advanced enough to use your inner guru. I will, however, outline some specific things you want to accomplish in your meditation sessions throughout this lifetime.

- seek ideas for your purpose,
- seek knowledge for your spiritual growth,
- seek ideas for new Kriya Serpent techniques,
- hold regular conversations with your inner guru,
- seek other spiritual advisors,
- seek downloads from the Akashic records,
- contemplate your previous lives and how they will guide you now,
- sit in stillness and contemplate "I am,"
- continue the separation of your Soul from your ego,
- eventually contact Celestial entities,
- seek higher planes of reality,
- astral projections,
- deeper states of consciousness,
- peer beyond the veil,

- manifest, and
- improve life state.

There is so much more, but you will know what and when you should pursue those things. I would give you a word of caution. Your purpose is why you are here, so do not get lost in the *Cosmos* at the expense of your purpose. There is so much to learn and to experience that you cannot do it all in a single lifetime, so pace yourself.

I would also urge you to stay more focused and spend a lot of time on a single thing before moving on to other things. You will not achieve mastery if you are constantly jumping from one thing to the next. I am a victim of that myself. I always want to know more, and sometimes I forget to master something before I move on.

From here on out, you are the captain of the ship on your spiritual journey through this wonderful Universe. Use your intuition, your inner guru and your spiritual guides to navigate. Our Creator gave you a mind, a spirit and a Soul imbued with powerful gifts to create your own future and your own world. The Universe is literally the only limit, and even that may not be a true limit.

If I had one directive to give you, spend as much time as you can in contemplation and meditation on your purpose. You'll find that when you do amazing ideas will pour forth into your mind, leading you to the fruition of your life's work. That is *why you are here,* after all.

Education

There are two aspects of your educational pursuits: *spiritual* and *intellectual.* The spiritual is obviously expanding your knowledge of the Universe, spiritual practices, beliefs and origins. The intellectual is all about your purpose. Whatever that purpose is, you need to understand all aspects of it to become an expert on those things.

We are endowed with intelligence so we can become experts at all facets of existence. Throughout our lifetimes, we build up a cache of experience and expertise in various areas of life. Eventually, that knowledge serves us when we ascend to the Soul state and manifest the creators we will become.

In this lifetime, you need to become an expert in the areas related to your purpose. Based on my experience, I predict your existing knowledge and aptitudes already qualify you for your purpose, though maybe not specifically. I wrote novels when I was called to service, and I translated that into writing this book. My background in engineering will help me when I need to build the infrastructure for the blueprint, and as a teacher, I am equipped to teach others this yoga and how to pursue their own purpose.

I suspect your innate talents and knowledge can also apply to your particular purpose. However, like me, you do not know everything you need to know to accomplish your purpose immediately. Maybe for some, that might be the case, but doubtful. Learning is a lifelong pursuit.

Let's talk *spiritual* education first, and then dive into education for your purpose in more detail. Spiritually, you will continue to grow and learn as you continue to practice Kriya Serpent Yoga, but there is so much more out there. I will not direct you into any specific thing because I believe at this stage you will have your own intuition to guide you. But let me at least give you some areas to consider:

- physics and consciousness,
- origins of humanity,
- origins of religions and beliefs,
- history of extraterrestrial intelligence on earth,

- CE-5 Contact Protocol,
- life of Jesus (contentious I know, but later in this practice you will understand why),
- Kriya Yoga and yogic history,
- the Vedas of Hinduism,
- Buddhism,
- chakras and auras,
- energy healing,
- manifesting,
- schools of mysteries,
- crystal energy,
- breathing,
- walking and dance meditation,
- sound, matter and states of consciousness,
- psychedelic substances and planes of reality,
- noetic sciences (telepathy, telekinesis, remote viewing, divination),
- physical yoga,
- astral projection,
- lucid dreaming and spiritual practice,
- vibraturgy,
- consciousness in the material sciences, and
- conscious states through sound (binaural, hemi-synch).

I realize this is a long list and far from comprehensive. We are talking the rest of your life, so start out slowly letting your intuition, inner guru, spirit guides, or self-interests guide you. It is likely few of us can know it all in a single lifetime, but over many lifetimes, it will accumulate through our Souls as we evolve.

For your purpose, where do you start? As I mentioned earlier, you likely have many of the required skills to begin your purpose already, but there will be more involved. I think it is best to help you by looking at it as an engineer might.

First, you must break down your purpose into smaller parts. For me, I broke it down into the following, starting with the big ideas and then expanding. When I was in engineering, this was called functional decomposition:

- Awaken new humans
    - learn and practice new yoga,
    - write books about new yoga,
    - create new author persona,
    - create new book series,
    - create new author website, and
    - create book series online forum.
- Build Blueprint
    - write book about it as basic framework,
    - start non-profit,
    - create website,
    - start podcast,
    - create business proposal,
    - create 1-, 5- and 10-year plans, and
    - generate income and donations.

Okay, there is more, but you get the idea. Start with your main ideas and break them down over time into their constituent parts. Only then can you identify the areas where you lack knowledge or skills to accomplish the task. For me, starting a non-profit was a big black hole, so that is an area I have been learning more about.

If you are a business savvy person, you recognize this as the start of project planning. As you continue to practice Kriya Serpent Yoga, the ideas about your purpose will flow freely, and this process will take shape. Over time, you will have a solid idea of what needs to be done and what you'll need to make it happen. That will guide your educational pursuits.

I want to say one thing about this. Your purpose is not something you will do all by yourself. You will need other people, resources, etc., to complete it, so don't get stressed. The key is you want to be the expert on most of the areas directly related to your purpose, and look at your role as architect, engineer and manager for your purpose. You will drive it, but others will help you build it.

So what is it you will build? Let's look at another example to further illustrate what I am talking about.

Let's say the purpose given to you is to change the structure of democracy so that it works for all people rather than a select few (wealthy). Simple enough, or is it? What do you know about democracy right now? How does our government work? What is the difference between Executive, Legislative, Judicial and Bureaucratic arms of the government? How do you change them to fulfill your purpose?

Okay, I picked a big one, and you would not likely be given this purpose unless you already had knowledge. But you get the point. You must be knowledgeable about the areas you are being tasked to change. So perhaps you should know about all the current and past types of democracies on our planet. What was good about them, and what was wrong with them? How do they work? How can you change them? Without these answers, your purpose will never be fulfilled.

But must it be fulfilled in this lifetime? Not necessarily. It is all about understanding the here and now, charting a path to a future and getting the ball rolling to move towards that future. But knowledge is fundamental to those foundational steps. Without it, you are flying blind.

To inspire you, imagine being the architect that designs the future democracy for humanity, then you reincarnate two hundred years later and lead the revolution for that new democracy. You get the picture, you may not make it happen in this lifetime, but you should have a good start on it before you pass on.

Positive Life State

No one can be successful if they are constantly battling a negative life state. Addictions, chronic illness, poor physical shape and constant psychological issues will always keep us from being the best we can. For some of you, this may be a problem in your life right now. You must reverse your negative life state so that you can become the person who will change the world.

I cannot give you all the ways upon which you can accomplish this, but accomplish it you must. If you do not, your progress will be extremely hindered and slowed to the point of stopping altogether. Most people, when faced with such an uphill battle, give up. You would be in good company if that is what you do.

But is that why you started this journey, to give up? I will borrow a line from a show I watched: *there is no halfway with this*. If you started this all the way back in the Introductory Level and made it all the way here, then you are committed. No halfway—*all the way!*

While we may not view it this way, it is part of your spiritual growth. We are whole organisms, not just our minds and Souls. Our body has an enormous bearing on our life state, which deeply impacts our psychological state and our ability to think, operate and grow. You must overcome these obstacles.

Meditation can certainly overcome many things in your personal life, but some will require physical interventions like counseling, medication and exercise. Seek what you need to overcome these impediments and you will be enriched with a better life state and spiritual growth. The tools are there, but no one except you can make you use of them.

Manifesting

This is a curious area that has recently become a bit of a social trend around the world. I am no expert, but I want to discuss it to give you some idea of what it is and how it works.

First, we need to understand our Creator wants only good things for us. Things that will help us experience life, grow spiritually and evolve into the highest form we can. Based on that premise, we can receive earthly things to assist us in our evolution. Yes, material things, though not strictly material things.

Now, as I have pursued my purpose, the Divine has cleared paths for me to make my pursuit easier. Yes, there are real things occurring in my life that I didn't ask for but have been directly beneficial for my work in the service of our Creator.

Manifesting is all about asking, though some may call it praying. Our thoughts dictate the world we see and experience, and that is the key to manifesting. You have heard about positive thinking before, and maybe, like me, you were skeptical at best and cynical at worst.

I must admit, early in my life, I always classified myself as an optimistic cynic. That meant I was hopeful things would go well, but was pretty sure they wouldn't. This is negative thinking, and it is a type of risk aversion. Expect the worst and hope for the best. This was my way of never feeling surprised and disappointed when things didn't go right.

It is negative because it sets the expectation that things will go wrong, thus laying a foundation for things to manifest wrong. Our thoughts become manifest, so we must first control them before we can ask for those things we desire. It is not the asking, but the belief that they will become manifest that makes the magic.

This concept is mentioned throughout the Bible, but most miss that concept because they are risk-adverse people who think negatively. We are conditioned, and breaking that conditioning is critical to bringing forth what we desire. Many of the new humans are not crippled by this conditioning, so they manifest far easier than the rest of us.

I am slowly de-programming myself from that earlier mindset, but admit it is difficult for this leopard to change his spots. Once you realize the truth of reality and your role within it, it becomes easier to think positive and live without fear, but it takes time. I will present a basic manifesting technique and let you see how it works. If it doesn't seem to work, your thinking may be the culprit.

If you are like me, you already know what I am talking about, and when you meet someone who is not like you, you feel annoyed. Yeah, I get that, but our reality is what we think, so start changing your thinking if you want to change your reality. This is a basic tenet of Buddhism.

Your Purpose

> *But beware of this about callings: they may not lead us where we intended to go or even where we want to go. If we choose to follow, we may have to be willing to let go of the life we already planned and accept whatever is waiting for us. And if the calling is true, though we may not have gone where we intended, we will surely end up where we need to be.*
> **Steve Goodier**

Beware of callings, indeed! They can be troubling because they will, by necessity, disrupt our existing plans for life. For many, however, their life was on a course to nowhere, so the disruption is welcome.

In either case, a calling is a major event in one's life and cannot be unseen or un-experienced afterwards. So does that mean you must throw away your existing life and start anew, chasing down the goal you have now accepted?

As a parent of two children, I am very aware of my parental responsibilities and the effort required in meeting those demands. It's hard to find the time to write and pursue my purpose, but it can be done. And ultimately, that is where free will comes into play. Not in saying no, but in figuring out how to make it work.

We are called to service, but how, when and where are up to us. Do not trade in a more *traditional* human life only to pursue your Divine purpose unless that is truly what you want. If you want children, have children. If you want marriage, get married. If you want to own a home, buy a home.

The Divine does not want you to miss out on life simply to pursue your purpose. After all, we are all here to experience life. Even Lahiri Mahasaya had a family when he was called to his purpose to revive Kriya Yoga and introduce it to the mainstream public.

I hope you can see why I am not expecting you to run away from life and lock yourself in a monastery, taking vows of silence, chastity, or poverty. No, I expect you to live life like it is the best thing you have ever been given, because it is!

Your purpose is not your life—*your life is your purpose*. That means live and find the means upon which you can fulfill your service while living. You have been given incredible gifts (Divine gifts), learn to harness that power and apply it to both your life and your purpose. Whatever life you have or want, live it to the fullest. With Divine guidance and your incredible gifts, you can make it all work.

When I accepted my call to service, I stipulated I would not give up my life to pursue it. My children, my material possessions I worked so hard to achieve, and all the fun activities I enjoy are important to me, and I will not give them up. I was simply told, don't give them up.

In return for my service, I was promised a long life. I am happy about that, because I love this life. I was also told that fast is not better than quality. The exact words were "Don't do it fast, do it right." They are correct. I have time. Don't rush it, but do it right.

This is an important point to make. We all lack patience when we are young; it is a hallmark of youth. That is fine, but not at the expense of breaking our ideals or ruining our lives. We don't take up arms to make the world change, but we assist the world in changing. We don't cancel things we disagree with, but show another path and encourage others to try it.

The Divine is on our side. Help will be provided when needed, and we will initiate this change without violence, hatred, or coercion. We don't need the things we are replacing in the new age. They are the old baggage from the old world of Homo sapiens, and they will disappear. It is time for the rise of Homo illustratus.

Homo sapiens do not want to perish from this earth, but neither did Homo habilis nor Neanderthals. But perish they did, for evolution proceeds no matter how much we may rail against it.

We are all blessed, for we have incarnated at the end of an age and have been called to service to help in this evolutionary shift. *Whoa!* I mean, truly mind blowing, but that is why we don't have to move fast and use outdated modes of thinking to make it happen. It will happen, and we can help this transition navigate the archaic world crumbling around us.

I outlined your educational needs for your purpose and showed you a basic process for planning your purpose. Functional decomposition is the first step in understanding the scope and scale of your purpose. From there, you will break it down into smaller components until you reach tasks that are easy to complete.

Project management is too large to put into this book, and that is basically what you are doing. Your purpose is your project, and you need to manage it from the idea stage into implementation. You will complete all the required steps within this lifetime, or perhaps several lifetimes, depending on the scope of your purpose.

At this level, achieve the following as a minimum before proceeding further:

1. document the main ideas of your purpose,
2. functionally decompose the ideas into smaller pieces,
3. continue this process and identify educational needs,
4. identify required resources, and
5. begin the process of acquiring resources and education.

Simple, yet an effective starting point. You will learn along the way, and adjust your efforts as needed. I will write additional books that contain more specific steps and processes after I have gone through them myself in pursuit of my purpose.

Kriya Serpent

This objective skill is interesting. I will not pretend to know anything about ashrams, temples, or other religious workings as I have lived my life outside those inner sanctums. However, because I was given a yoga technique to release into the world, I must discuss what this means without the traditional trappings of religious doctrine and practice.

First, and this is very important, this book is the only acceptable word on Kriya Serpent Yoga. I am the only one to receive this gift, and I have regular contact with the person from whom I received it. I will reveal more about Kriya Serpent Yoga's origins in future books, but for now, I am the WORD on Kriya Serpent Yoga.

Now, having said all that, this is a practice that will, out of necessity, have to change and grow to meet the ever-changing needs of the new humans manifesting. Neither I nor anyone else can predict what those needs are yet, though I can let my imagination soar if I think about it.

I already told you I am currently working with one of my spirit guides on what I will call Lucid Serpent, where practitioners will enter the dream state during meditation without having to "fall" asleep and wait for that stage of dreaming where lucidity occurs.

This may seem like pie in the sky, but I have semi-achieved it multiple times as of the writing of this book, and I have been assured it can be done, so I will continue to work on it because it will play a significant role in the future of Kriya Serpent Yoga. I believe there is an untapped area for spiritual growth and power within this lucid state, and those who already practice traditional lucid dreaming know what I am talking about. Now imagine becoming lucid at will, and you get the idea.

This practice will be constantly evolving, and I firmly believe many of you will play a role in that evolution. However, I do not want a patchwork collection of techniques claiming to be Kriya Serpent Yoga trying to usurp our role in humanity's evolution simply for personal profit. We don't need that kind of greed in our efforts—greed is Homo sapiens.

Because of this, as this practice evolves, there will be an official process for submitting new techniques which will be reviewed by a select group of practitioners before approval. If it is approved, it will be added into this official book. If you see something claiming to be Kriya Serpent but it is not published by me, Agni Lakshya, it is a fake and should be disregarded.

This will grow into a spiritual practice for all humans eventually, but new humans will benefit first as they use it for their purpose while ushering in the new age of humanity. Everything within Kriya Serpent Yoga must be focused towards that purpose only—for now. In the future, all humanity will benefit from this practice.

So how does this affect you? You will learn a lot of things through this practice and might even learn new techniques that benefit you. I am telling you, as an advanced practitioner, you should explore new things and see what integrating them into your practice does. If you receive instructions during your meditation on a new technique, try it out and if it works well for you, write it down and send it in.

I want you to expand your own practice and explore how this practice can be extended to assist all practitioners, so don't keep it to yourself when new ideas and techniques come to mind. At the time I am writing this book, the process for submissions is nothing more than an idea, but by the time this is published, there should be a formal process on my website, so check there for details. All who submit techniques that are approved will be given full credit.

As we enter the new age, we will all play a role in shaping humanity by providing tools to accomplish this transformation. Kriya Serpent Yoga is one of those tools, and I look forward to seeing how each of you contributes to its continual evolution. As we move forward, building a community where we can share ideas and inspiration will be a cornerstone of our practice.

We will have no ashrams or temples, but we will have a social network of fellow new humans to help each other rebuild this world for the next millennium.

Journaling

While I could have introduced this at an earlier level, an advanced practitioner must document their journey. If you read this book in its entirety before starting your journey, then document your entire journey from Level 1 through Level 4 and beyond. Journaling is a fantastic way to record your growth and spiritual evolution.

At this advanced level, it is imperative you journal all your experiences. There are many reasons for journaling, but the most important is to track your progression, recording the most significant events and experiences. You will appreciate having the record to refer to in the future, and it will pass on as a legacy to those who may pick up your torch.

This was common not so long ago, but in the age of electronics, hand written journals have become quite rare except for writers or scientists. Perhaps you are not a writer, but down the road you may wish to document your story to inspire others. If we are beacons for all to see, then let us write our stories so that they may learn from us.

Though you needn't invest a lot on a journal, if you want something that is nice, easy to write on, and contains a placeholder ribbon and can be held shut with latch or band, then assume an approximate cost of $20–$30 USD for a standard one.

Depending on size and the creativity of the cover, they can range even higher in cost. I find I prefer the blank, lined journals where I fill in everything. Some may prefer one with dates already pre-printed on the pages. The problem with that is you are then limited to whatever page size it is for each day. I have had some entries which have spanned 5–6 pages.

I also find writing the experiences a great way to review and solidify my memory of events, and it allows me to write questions I may ponder about them. You will be surprised how some experiences are like a puzzle to be solved. But that is the work of our spiritual growth, well worth documenting for posterity and your own reference.

Though I haven't done it yet, I have often wondered what patterns may be revealed if I were to sit down and read through everything in the order that they occurred. There has been plenty of mystery in my own experiences that may hide patterns I haven't fully understood.

I found patterns that helped me understand more recent events after reviewing experiences I had throughout my life before starting my spiritual path. Memory fades over time, but pen and paper last many lifetimes. In the journaling section below, I outline ideas for how to document your experiences. I have a simple but effective technique.

Traditional Techniques

Manifesting

This technique originates from the school of mysteries. It encapsulates the basic idea mentioned most while discussing this topic. Your state of mind is critical to this process, so you may need to prepare yourself mentally before you try.

Time is not something controllable in this technique, therefore the right mind is critical. When I say right mind, I mean that when you do this, you must know it will be done. Not maybe, or not sure. Not, I don't believe in such things, but absolutely positively know this will work. Some may call that faith, but I prefer calling it knowing.

Let me give you an example. Many claim they have faith, but what they mean by that is they do all the things they were taught through their religion and hope it will work. That is faith for most people, and when they say believe, they really mean hope.

Knowing is like taking an ice cube from the freezer and setting it out in the blistering sun on your driveway. You know it is going to melt, not that you hope it will melt. Once you set the ice cube down, you know it will melt and the resulting water will evaporate in the sunshine. *Works every time!*

But asking for something from an invisible Creator who you are just now beginning to fully understand? Well, that feels more like hope, and there is the problem. You cannot hope it will manifest, you know it will. This is much easier said than done if you are conditioned like me.

Most people harbor doubts and concerns, and if you suffer from certain psychological issues like anxiety and depression, then it is nearly impossible to avoid doubt. It is ingrained within us, and that is why the world we manifest is riddled with negativity and uncertainty. That was me, and I still struggle. Have no fear, practice Kriya Serpent Yoga, and those doubts will soon melt away like the ice cube in the scorching sun.

If you are not riddled with doubt and fully know your Creator will assist you, then this is your chance to manifest. Henry Ford, the creator of Ford Motors, once said that whether you think you can do a thing or you think you cannot do a thing, you are right. That applies here.

You will manifest during the meditating section of your daily practice. It requires focus and visualization, and you should have thought through exactly what you want and what it would look like once you receive it. Have it scripted in your mind before you start your daily session.

Keep it within the realm of your purpose to begin with and keep it a single request. First, ask yourself if there is no other way to attain this? If you haven't even tried to accomplish it on your own, then perhaps you are looking for handouts. Remember, God helps those who help themselves, so try everything first before reaching out for Divine intervention.

1. Sit in meditation.
2. Complete Serpent Fire and Tantric Variation.
3. Give thanks and gratitude to our Creator.
4. Meditate in the stillness of the gray sphere for 5 minutes as you sink further into deeper states of consciousness.
5. With intense focus, visualize the desire whose manifestation you wish. Your visualization should be clear, precise and as lifelike as possible. Imagine you are part of it and visualize all details of what you look like and feel like. You should see how it will change your life and

the pursuit of your purpose. Your visualization should be so real that you feel like it has already happened. Details and realism are critical.

6. Once your visualization is as crystal clear as you can make it, inhale deeply through your nose and hold the air in your lungs for 30 seconds.
7. Exhale the air as you mentally say: *Thank you God for manifesting this desire, it is done.*
8. Forget your visualization and do not think upon your desire again with the certain knowledge that it will manifest.

For practical purposes, I will give you an example. Let's assume you need to visit a distant city for research for your purpose or to collaborate or meet people who are instrumental to your purpose. The problem is you don't have the means to make that trip happen. You have tried to raise money through many methods and have come up blank. You need Divine intervention.

When you visualize this request, see yourself arriving at the city, locating the information or people you need and the emotions and sensations that you will experience while there. You should also visualize the results and how they contribute to your overall purpose.

Focus and visualization are critical in this. Think of your visualization as an image you are attaching to an email request. If it is blurry, confusing, not concise or so generic it could mean anything, then whoever reads the email will not understand what you are asking for. Be explicit and visualize clearly as though it were real.

If afterwards you are not sure it will happen, but you only hope it will, then it will probably fail. You know that it will happen because you did everything correctly, and it is for your purpose. The Creator wants to help you with your purpose, so of course it will happen. Have no doubts, it will be done.

Millions have used this successfully because they are using it for their own spiritual growth, the growth or help of others, or to pursue their life's purpose. It will work for you, so "know" it will work, don't hope.

I have one last comment. Do not make requests on how your desire should be fulfilled, only make the desire known. How will be up to the Divine, and it may happen in ways you never even imagined. In our example, instead of visualizing an airline flight to the city, just visualize arriving at the city and everything else that is part of the trip.

When it manifests, it could be someone who tells you they have an extra ticket to travel to that city, or it could be an opportunity to join a group who are bussing to the destination, or a ride-share. You might find a raffle you can buy to win a trip to that location. Who knows how it might manifest? You might just suddenly come into money to pay for the trip. The *how* is up to the Divine.

Know it will happen and that it will happen at the most opportune time for you and your spiritual needs. Even if you believe your purpose is too great to accomplish, you will be surprised how much "additional" or "coincidental" help will keep coming your way. And if need be, you can now ask for it directly.

Journaling

The following is a list of things you definitely want to write in your journal:

- Date/Time. I find time less important, but some may disagree.
- Techniques you added into your session if different from your usual regimen.
- All unusual effects during a session or any large variations in energy.

- Visions, lights, images, ideas and downloads.
- Conversations:
    - who? what? where? how?
    - Guidance or special knowledge,
    - warnings or intimidating commentary, and
    - was Divine love presented?
- Dreams the night before or night after.
- Lucid dreams and how they were triggered.
- Different states of consciousness.
- Astral projections.
- New physical body sensations.
- Questions you have about your experiences.
- Descriptions of the people you meet during your session.
- States of bliss or religious significance.
- Emotions you feel if different than normal.
- All past traumas and karma that surface.
- Results of new techniques.
- Premonitions of places, people, or events.
- Feelings of dread or impending doom.
- Things that happen later that you believe may correlate with experiences in your session.
- Feedback from others if you discuss it with them.
- Physical visions (see with your eyes) or other physical sensations without an obvious source.
- Any healing or improvement in preexisting conditions.

This is a lot, but you won't be writing all of this every single day. In fact, I recommend you only journal on days when something new, different, or unusual occurs. If your daily regimen is uneventful or ordinary, then no need to journal it. Starting out, most experiences will relate to your purpose while in deeper states of consciousness or visions. Later, more interesting things will manifest and you may be journaling more regularly.

There are periods where I have journaled every day for a couple of weeks, and then periods where I do not journal for a few weeks. It will depend on your journey and where it leads you. If it is something you think about all day after your session ends, then you likely want it in your journal.

Since my entries are rather long, I find it useful to log a separate entry into another journal as a *timeline* of the main events or experiences. If I go back through and need more clarity, I can access the original journal entry by the date in the timeline journal.

I use the following headers for my journal entries as needed:

- Date and Time,
- Dreams,
- Meditation, and
- Inner Dialogues.

For my timeline journal, it is simply a date followed by a brief description of the experience or event. You want the timeline to be simple and concise, though sometimes my entries are long because a lot happened.

As you begin this practice of logging your spiritual journey, you will eventually come up with your own style and techniques. Do what works best for you, but make sure it is readable for others. If something happens to you, you want others to easily decipher your writing and learn from it.

You should physically number each journal and make sure your name and contact information is on it in case it should get lost. This is your data, and you would love for it to find its way back home in the event it is lost. Now, for most of us, it never leaves home, but you never know. I often take mine on trips to make sure I can document anything that happens in my practice when I am away from home. If I wait until I return from the trip, the recollection will not be as good.

I also write in an *idea* journal. Since you have found your purpose, you will think about it nearly every day (daily for me). I keep a small, pocket size journal with me to jot down ideas, areas to explore and relationships or contacts related to my purpose. Having a small and quick place to jot them down is indispensable for keeping up with the steady flow of information coming at you.

These ideas often come at very unusual times. I have them at work, conferences, shopping, vacation, etc. I don't always have my idea journal with me, but I usually do since ideas flow regularly. Jotting it down as soon as you can will keep it fresh and prevent you from losing it during your busy life.

Journaling can be a major part of this practice once you reach the advanced level, and you will never regret doing it if only for your autobiography later on. You never know. Because of the incredible nature of what we are doing, I believe we should all leave an autobiography as inspiration for others who follow us. Paramahansa Yogananda did, and it inspired me and many others.

I try to journal as soon as I can after whatever session I need to document. However, to write a journal entry can sometimes take a while, so if you need to wait a day or two, don't get too distressed as long as your memory of it is still fresh. I try to do mine while drinking coffee before work immediately after my meditation session, but sometimes life gets in the way and can push that timeline out.

Another great time to journal is in the evening before bed. I sometimes do that because of time constraints, and it is nice to have the day to reflect on the experiences and see what comes from those reflections. Either way, write it in your journal as soon as possible.

If you haven't had anything to journal about for a while, create a journal entry discussing that and pose questions about why that might be the case and what you can change or do about it. If nothing is happening, that is worth writing about. Otherwise, you may stagnate, and that is worth writing about and figuring out why so you can prevent it.

One last journal I keep is for the new techniques I learn or try out. It is a manual for all the techniques I have in my arsenal. While this book you are reading contains many of these techniques, there are many more I have not shared or that are still under development. Another journal for these can be useful if you decide to try your hand at developing specific techniques or when you learn new ones during meditation.

Of course, all of this journaling can be done online, and I am not advocating that you don't. However, technology is great when it works, and when it doesn't, then what? I came from the tech industry in my earlier years and still keep in touch with my tech roots regularly. However, I have not found a useful tool that is easy to access and easy to use the way I need to.

That may change over time, and may even be a mission we take on in the future. But for now, I am an advocate for the original pen and paper journaling. No electricity required. If you are savvier and find an online tool that works for you, please use it and report your experiences with it in the forums on our website.

Kriya Serpent Techniques

Serpent Star

This technique was given to me in an unusual way. I was doing my meditation as usual and had just finished Ujjayi Breathing and was about to begin Serpent Fire. As I went through each cycle, there was no Kundalini rising, though I could feel the energy within me building. I was confused and assumed my body was tired, sick, or had some other problem.

I finished Serpent Fire with no Kundalini and was about to do the Tantric Variation to raise my Kundalini when a vision within my mind's eye arose. There was a ball of energy in front of me, like a sun the size of a football or basketball. I was mesmerized. It was just like looking into the sun through special telescopes. You could see the energy swirling in arcs and loops within.

Energy radiated out from it, warming the front of my body. The light was blinding, but it didn't hurt my eyes. I was amazed. A voice told me to concentrate on this tiny star, focusing only on it as I felt the energy within my body flow out into the orb. I visualized the energy arcing out of my arms, legs and torso, flowing into the orb as its light intensified.

I was mesmerized by the feeling of the energy flowing through the conduit of my body and didn't know how much time had passed. Finally, the voice told me to extend my arms towards the orb and grab it with both hands (mental visualization). I felt the enormous energy surging through it, warm and inviting.

I was instructed to swallow the orb. Yes, weird as that sounds, I visualized swallowing the orb, its energy filling my mouth, my head, my throat and finally my chest. I was told to focus the orb into my Heart chakra where it would live throughout the day. It was like having a warm hug of love with you all day. *Amazing!*

I was instructed to focus my thoughts on this orb in my chest throughout the day and feed off the loving energy that it would radiate within me, so I did. I was cautioned I should do nothing that would ground me, as I needed to spend the day in this elevated energy state. By the time dinner rolled around, the energy had nearly dissipated, but the warm feelings it had radiated still flowed through me.

As mentioned earlier, you will know when you are ready for Serpent Star when you have a meditation where there is no Kundalini. Don't force it. It will happen on its own and you cannot mistake it. Once it does, follow these steps:

1. Sit in meditation.
2. Complete all techniques up to meditating stage.
3. If Kundalini DOES NOT rise, complete the following during your meditating session.
4. Visualize a glowing orb of energy in front of you. Make it crystal clear and bright so you feel the warmth from it.
5. Focus on the energy, watching it build from the energy within your Serpent Fire practice. Visualize energy arcing off you and all objects around you. It is like the orb is absorbing all the energy within the room. Feel it flow into the ball, intensifying to blinding proportions.
6. Once it is nearly blinding, grab it with both hands (mentally) and feel the energy within it.
7. Visualize swallowing it and feel the effects as it moves from your mouth through your head and down into your chest. Focus on moving the orb into you Heart chakra and feel it radiate energy from within.
8. Complete your meditating session as you see fit.
9. Do not ground yourself for the rest of the day, and constantly return your focus to the orb to feel its loving energy that will nourish you.

It is hard to describe the feeling of this star within you. I guess the best I can do is say you will feel more love and compassion for everything than on an ordinary day. For me, these days are the best day of the week. It is like nothing can go wrong and you feel as though the Creator is with you all day. It is an amazing sensation, and I believe it attunes your body to all the subtle energies around you. This is an advanced technique, and if it is difficult to accomplish, you might not be ready for it.

It can amplify your anxiety operating at this energy level well above a normal baseline, even for those who do Kundalini regularly. When the anxiety creeps in, focus on the orb and feel the love it radiates, and that will eliminate the anxiety.

While I never received any great new ideas or visions about my purpose on these days, I am happier than I am most other days, and in a very peaceful state. Pretty remarkable considering I am a teacher of teenagers. Once you reach this level of practice, I am excited to hear about your experiences. The website will have a forum for you to share these experiences.

Remember, we cannot walk around in this heightened energy state every day, so please only do Serpent Star once a week, and only if your Kundalini does not rise during one of your daily sessions. During one of my normal weeks, Wednesdays are typically Serpent Star day.

However, I should note that it doesn't happen every single week. That is okay. Our Kundalini will ebb and flow as does our natural biological and ethereal systems. We do not want to force anything, but enter each meditation session with fresh eyes. If it doesn't happen this week, it will happen during another week. I am not concerned because I know it will happen when I will benefit most.

Crystal Serpent

I was on the fence about calling this Crystal Serpent, but then I realized I learned this all on my own. Okay, there was some Divine inspiration, but no crystal expert. Therefore, I am taking ownership of this technique as my own creation.

Before I list the steps, I want to take a moment to discuss something fascinating which has some applicability to this technique. If we think of an energy flow as rotating, then it can either rotate clockwise or anti-clockwise. In our spiritual work, we want our energy flowing clockwise, as this is in tune with much of the natural world.

Anti-clockwise isn't bad. It is simply counter to the prevailing flows around you. Because of that, anti-clockwise rotation of energy will build a lot of energy in a short amount of time through the friction between the different flows.

I have a technique called Serpent Lightning, and as the name might imply, it is powerful. I deemed it too powerful for this book, and I only use it rarely. If this level is advanced, then Serpent Lightning belongs at the next level after this. It uses anti-clockwise energy flow to build energy up. It was taught to me after I asked for a technique which would help me pierce the veil that hides those in the beyond.

While I had very serious reasons for wanting to do this (not related to my wife, by the way), it was too much energy and stole from me that which we are trying to cultivate. While I entered a higher dimension where I met amazing entities, I did not achieve what I set out to do. Look for it in later books after there are enough practitioners ready for it.

All of this is to say that Crystal Serpent depends on a clockwise energy flow that you sense and feel. When you connect with your crystals, sense a flow moving from your left hand to your right hand and back again, forming a giant loop rotating clockwise if you were looking down from above.

If you do not have that clockwise flow, this may be problematic and may prevent you from clearing chakras. You may try to reverse the direction of the flow mentally, but I cannot verify that will work. My crystals were clockwise from the moment I picked them up.

1. Sit in meditation.
2. Complete all techniques up to the meditating state.
3. Pick up each crystal wand and hold in closed fist with flat end perpendicular to your palm and pointed end sticking out above your fist.
4. Place the center of your thumbprints on the pointed end of the crystal and hold your arms at a ninety degree bend as you rest your closed fists on or near your knees. This completes the circuit where you should feel that clockwise flow of energy passing through the air from left to the

right hand, then through the body and the chest cavity back to the left hand.

5. Sit in silence for a few minutes feeling the energy flow. It should flow through the Heart chakra as it completes the circuit.
6. Inhale deeply through your nose while mentally intoning the "Ah" sound.
7. Exhale through your nose while mentally intoning the "Ohm" sound and focus the *crystal energy* into your Base chakra for the entirety of the exhalation.
8. Repeat steps 6–7 two (2) more times for a total count of three (3).
9. Repeat steps 6–8 for each of the remaining chakras in the order listed below:
    - Sacral,
    - Solar Plexus,
    - Heart,
    - Throat, and
    - Third Eye:
        - center of head first,
        - forehead point between eyes second (Bhrumadhya), and
    - crown.
10. Since you are channeling your Kundalini through the point on the forehead between your eyes, I have added this as though it were a main chakra.
11. After completing the chakras, do it again three (3) times with the energy flowing throughout all etheric channels in your body.
12. Put your crystals down and complete your meditating session.

It is possible that during your clearing session, your Kundalini rises. That is okay. Just let it surge as you channel it as normal, then return to whatever clearing you were doing. You do not need beads for this since you are only counting three times for each chakra, and after a few practices, you will do it automatically.

When you are done, you will feel a noticeable difference within your entire body. Like I said before, *breath mint* for the body. This cleansing is only necessary once a week and should not be done more often than that. While I do not know what effects it might have if done daily, my intuition tells me it might interfere with some of the tuning we are trying to accomplish, since it is equivalent to resetting each chakra.

Having said this, if you feel negative, as though you picked up some negative energy somewhere along the way, do this and cleanse yourself of that negative energy sooner rather than later. I pick up negative energy all the time from people, places, objects and dead people (don't ask).

However, I rarely have to cleanse more than once a week. Pick a day and make it your routine. I recommend either Saturday or Sunday when you are relaxed and less likely to run into negative energy as you might during the work week. I do it on Sunday when I complete my mystery school lessons. I figure if I am learning something new, best to have clean energy to work with.

Daily Regimen

You plan your meditation sessions at this stage, but here is a recommended weekly regimen including the new techniques:

<u>Weekly Regimen (60–90 minutes total per day):</u>

1. Nadi Shodhana (Mon–Sun): 6–12 counts,
2. Ujjayi Breathing (Mon–Sun): 12–24 counts,
3. Serpent Fire (Mon–Sun): 24–36 cycles,
4. Tantric Fire Variation (Mon–Sun): 3 counts,

5. Serpent Star (Wed): 1 count,
6. Crystal Serpent (Sun): 1 count,
7. Meditating (Mon–Sun): How long is up to you, and
8. Journaling (Mon–Sun): As needed.

I put meditating after Serpent Star and Crystal Serpent to indicate you should spend time in deep meditation after those techniques. Serpent Star will often place you into excellent meditation states, so do not ignore those opportunities. Even Crystal Serpent can re-activate chakras once the negative energy has been cleansed, so you may experience Kundalini afterwards.

The counts I have listed are based on my practice but will give you an overall session between 60–90 minutes. Clearly, choose the counts that work best for you and fit your time requirements specifically. Again, you can do this once or twice a day, depending on your availability and desire. For most busy people, once is sufficient.

As noted earlier, Serpent Star and Crystal Serpent should only be done once in a week. If you meditate twice a day, do these techniques in your earlier session to get the most benefit. Never do both on the same day as they will interfere with each other and you won't receive the full benefit from each.

Your meditating session will expand within the advanced level, so explore which aspects of meditating provide the best experience. I would not integrate too many meditating techniques into a single week, but a couple of different ones you alternate may be beneficial. A lot of work can be accomplished during the meditating sessions, so do not ignore it.

I am always trying to figure out which things to accomplish during my meditating session, but too often I am interrupted with specific things I must deal with. That is fine, since these things are very much related to my purpose and spiritual growth. However, I still like the stillness as a default, and you should keep that a weekly staple in your regimen. As you grow, your intuition will guide you.

The after-effects of your daily sessions will follow you throughout the day. SantataGamana believes, as I do, that paying particular attention to these after-effects is essential to your spiritual development. Do not disregard them, but actively engage with them, noting all the details, emotions and questions that arise.

Move on with your day, but pay attention to the emotions, feelings and behaviors you experience. Questions always arise, and you should seek to find answers for them. This is the spiritual work I talked about earlier, and you'll grow when you engage in that work.

You may experience incredible mystical events after meditation during your normal daily routines. I have experienced visions, states of bliss, Kundalini surges, resurfaced karma, premonitions, telepathy, empathic emotions and more. These will not be a regular part of your daily routine, but be prepared in the event they happen. It can be awkward at work, but a quick break to the restroom will provide you time to adjust or process as needed.

In subsequent books in this series, I will touch upon this more, but for now, be active in monitoring your overall transformation. Once you start down the path of your purpose, you will find it constantly occupies much of your thoughts throughout the day. It doesn't mean you cannot work or live your life, but it is always there as your mind continues to process it and devise new ideas and strategies.

Warnings, Suggestions and Side Effects

Because you have advanced in your practice to a point where you are now in charge of your journey, you must use your intuition and inner guru to guide you through your practice. I have spoken at length about this already, so I won't belabor the point.

However, be aware, you are not yet a *Master* of Kriya Serpent Yoga. The person who instructed me is a Master, and I think of myself as more of an Initiate, one step above an Acolyte which Levels 1–3 might represent.

I eschew titles, but some people cling to them. As an engineer and mathematics teacher, I prefer numbering rather than titles. You reach this level just as an Initiate in the Mystery schools might reach a similar level. This is level 4. If pressed, I would say there are at least a few more levels within this practice based on other lessons I have learned which you are not yet ready for.

As I learn and create new techniques, I will add additional levels to this practice. These additional levels will be released when I believe there are those who will benefit. This book will be a living book, and will change periodically as new things are approved and added. Do not fret, this is a lifetime practice, and I have given you powerful tools that would last you a lifetime. But there will be more.

The suggestions and warnings I give to you now are very much around the responsibility you now have based on achieving this vaulted level. While only an Initiate, you have been given tools that will unlock the entire Universe to you. In a manner of speaking, it is the equivalent of handing the keys of a Porsche to a 4-year-old. They could wreck and cause great destruction, or they could be the next future racer. Do not let humanity down as we are depending on you, new human.

Cultivate a Relationship with the Divine

Your purpose is from the Divine, and the help you need will come from the Divine, so cultivate a relationship with the Divine. Though I mentioned prayer as a regular part of your daily meditation, it should not be an afterthought or a ritual set of phrases you repeat until it means very little.

When you pray, think about all that has been given to you, not just material things, but spiritual things including this practice. This is a revelation of enormous magnitude, especially for those who have never had such a relationship before. Revel in the wonder of it all and show appropriate gratitude. It will not be wasted, and over time, you will cultivate a wonderful relationship with the Divine.

I always remember the Divine being with me in times of distress, but many do not, so relish this new opportunity and show your love and gratitude. Over time, you will establish regular conversations with the Divine, and you will grow and evolve into that which you were meant to become. This isn't about flashy magic and Cosmic entities, it is more often just about "I am." And "I am" a part of the Divine, just like you.

Be an Ambassador for Humanity

When the time arrives to hold conversations with entities within this realm and higher-level dimensions, you must conduct yourself as though an ambassador for humanity. They know we are young, so they are prepared for your awkward conversations.

Do not concern yourself wholly with how you think they perceive you, because they are ready to hear from those of us who are breaking out of our silent existence within the Cosmos. They want to see how we are changing, hoping to see a future where we join them as Universal citizens.

Be empathetic, loving and generous with your gratitude for whatever they offer, whether advice, knowledge, or simply love. Many have opened with an incredible shower of loving bliss when we first meet, and I suspect the same will be true for you. This tells you they mean no harm.

Many will know about humanity and its current state of affairs better than you do, so don't make the mistake of trying to school them about anything. They are far past us in spiritual and intellectual evolution, and we are the young children in the neighborhood. We learn from them, not the other way around.

If you feel uncomfortable, tell them you are not ready to engage with them and peacefully exit. Never be rude to anyone, even if they are rude to you. It will be rare if that happens, but it has happened to me. You are an ambassador for humanity and a servant of our Creator, so act appropriately.

As these special relationships expand, new opportunities will arise. Take advantage of these opportunities and expand beyond your ordinary life. New humans must forge onward into new frontiers, and while change is scary, it is how we grow and evolve. Without these relationships, humanity entering space could be treacherous. We need their wisdom to succeed beyond our planet.

Every third-dimensional species has gone through a similar evolution and understands where we are and what we need to do. Learn from them and use their knowledge to fulfill your purpose while enriching the evolution of humanity.

Having said all this, you do not need to engage. For some of you, they may not wish to engage you because they know where you are on your spiritual journey, and if you are not ready, they will not want to establish a relationship with you. That is okay. You have plenty to do to achieve your purpose, and these relationships will always wait for you to grow.

For others, your purpose may be to engage them. You will be pioneers in extraterrestrial intelligence. If that is you, take on the role with proper humility and learn all that you can. We can learn so much from them, shortening our own evolution and expansion into the Universe.

Ultimately, we must all be experts in the areas related to our purpose. Some will forge new frontiers, some will fix existing systems, and some will teach others about the new age that is coming. Embrace your purpose and be an ambassador for all to see.

Spread the Knowledge

The first edition of this book is the beginning of this practice in this time of human history. To spread it far and wide is not just part of your purpose but your mantle as a practitioner of Kriya Serpent Yoga for life. While the sale of these books generates necessary income for achieving my purpose, I do not care if people share their copy of this book with others.

Please do not copy the book, but lending your personal copy to another is fine. Some digital platforms allow sharing eBooks, and that is also acceptable. You can also spread this knowledge by telling people about it and sharing your experiences with the practice. That is the most effective method, as people may want to share in similar experiences.

If others show interest and you have the means, buy them their own copy as a gift and introduction to this practice. Even if they discover they are not interested, they may find someone else to whom they can pass on their copy. The key is to talk about it and share your own experiences so that we can reach all the new humans across the planet and get them reconnected with the Divine to find their purpose.

I am not savvy with social media, since I rarely have time for such things. However, I understand the positive aspects of social media, especially for spreading knowledge and experiences. Share your Kriya Serpent Yoga experiences with others through social media and share links to the website so they can learn about it themselves. It is an enormous world, but modern technology has shrunk it down tremendously.

If other organizations take an interest in Kriya Serpent Yoga, have them contact me through the website so we can discuss possible affiliations. It is not an uncommon practice between groups with similar interests and goals, so I am more than interested in hearing how we might benefit each other.

I understand reality and realize there may be critics who will malign our practice without ever cracking the book. Some will be dismissive because of their own beliefs, while others may denigrate it because of their ignorance and conditioned programming. Some will be purists who refuse to accept the evolving nature of yoga and humanity, refusing to let go of their authority to dictate what is right or wrong for the rest of us.

Do not engage with these people in any way other than to defend this practice peacefully. We need not prove ourselves to anyone, because that is not the purpose of Kriya Serpent Yoga. New humans will find it, and they will know the truth when they discover their purpose. Over time, those who attack it will simply fade away as the numbers of our practitioners steadily rise.

It is almost a guarantee some will attack us about sexuality and cult-like behaviors, which are simply false. We will have no temples, shrines, or places of worship. We will be an online community of new humans seeking the evolution of our Souls and the liberation of humanity. *That* is not a cult!

Anyone who disparages Kriya Serpent Yoga under the guise of being one of its practitioners will be denounced by me in communications to all practitioners. These individuals will not be tolerated as their behaviors could destroy our efforts.

I do not want to discourage open dialog about what we do, but we must conduct ourselves intelligently with wisdom at all times. We must model our spirituality and Divine love, conducting ourselves accordingly. As mentioned previously, we are servants of the Divine and ambassadors of humanity.

Beware of Narcissism

Narcissism is growing more rampant in our world lately, though it has always been here. With the advent of social media, it has morphed into a world-wide phenomenon. Ask yourself how many selfies you take in a single day? A week? A month? A year? Now ask yourself why.

Being self-indulgent and desiring good things for ourselves is not necessarily evil, but when it morphs into true narcissism, then you have a problem. Our role in this world is to help humanity evolve into the Divine entities we were created to become. There is no room for narcissism in that role.

We will discover incredible things, new people in the Universe, and the inherent powers within ourselves, but we must guard against these things turning us into narcissists. We are Bodhisattvas, those who put their own enlightenment after that of the rest of humanity. We are not practicing Kriya Serpent Yoga to glorify ourselves, especially at the expense of others.

This practice should cultivate a true love of all humanity, yes, even those who do not believe and are still living within the illusion. They are the ones we are here to assist. We will assist in their evolution because that is the stage in our own evolution where we currently find ourselves. We are teachers, architects and builders of the next millennium, not narcissists playing demigods with those less enlightened. That would be truly evil.

All tools and knowledge can be used for both good and evil, but don't fall into that trap. It is the trap of the false prophets and false saviors popping up as the new age comes into view. We work for our Creator only, and we are not demigods or anything other than servants.

I know the temptation of power. It has been offered to me multiple times, but I have always turned it down. I know what it is like to feel disdain and contempt for those who I once deemed intellectually inferior, but that is not our way. Our way is that of a humble servant, working peacefully for the betterment of humanity. Yes, we will benefit, too, but do not seek your own glory above others.

Every human on this planet has the Divine within them, and to deride them is to deride the Divine. To place yourself above them is to place yourself above the Divine, and that is blasphemy. Everyone has the potential to grow and evolve spiritually into their true self, but if we never give them the chance, they will never know it is possible.

We do not hold Kriya Serpent Yoga knowledge sacred. It is not only available to a chosen few based on some man-made criteria meant to sort, distort and oppress others for our own grandeur. We pass it on to all who seek it, and teach them the wisdom necessary to achieve their own transformation.

This is the difference between Homo illustratus and Homo sapiens. Homo illustratus will lead humanity into the age of the individual, where everyone is truly equal on all levels of reality. It will take time, but we are the keepers of that promise.

Worship the Creator

This may seem like a weird thing to say, but worship only our Creator. We all worship different things in our own way, but that is metaphorical worship rather than actual worship. There is only one Creator, and They have given us the gift of life, a Soul and a beautiful Universe in which to live, explore and experience.

The Creator is the only one who has brought this all together for us to enjoy, and everything else is but a part of that which They created. As quoted earlier, an Ocean can exist without the waves, but waves cannot exist without the Ocean. Everything in our Universe is but a wave within the Ocean of our Creator.

The history of humanity is replete with many deities, demigods, masters and enlightened ones, but they are all but parts of the whole, same as us. Yes, they are intelligent and powerful, but they are not different from us, just part of that which created us all. Learn from them, admire them, and show them the respect their vaulted state deserves, but do not worship them.

I have been asked multiple times to worship at the feet of others who have attained incredible evolutionary growth in the ethereal and physical planes, but I refuse them adamantly. Never have I disrespected them, but I will not worship them. I will not kneel before those who are not the Creator, and neither should you.

Right now, you are probably reading this thinking, I must be crazy, but I am not. While you may not fully understand what I am saying, a time will come when you will be asked to worship someone or something, and I am telling you, refuse them politely.

Your Soul is that part of the Creator within you. Know your Soul and you know the Creator. If not now, then eventually, as you practice Kriya Serpent Yoga. Once you make that connection, the Divine will never ask you to worship Them because you will do it naturally. As mentioned before, cultivate a relationship with the Divine and you will always know the truth.

On the Kriya Serpent Yoga website, there will eventually be a lot of conversation around this topic, and I look forward to your insights and experiences on this matter. For now, trust me and put no others above the Creator of this wonderful Universe.

Heal Yourself and Others

My last words of advice are about healing. I am not talking about physical healing, for that is another topic, but healing psychologically and spiritually. Not just for yourself, but others you have contact with.

I find it all too easy to worry about myself at all times, wondering if my health is okay. Am I doing the right things spiritually? Can I do more for my purpose? It can be all-encompassing. But as I mentioned before, we are not monks in a monastery but living beings with a modern world life and all its trappings.

Those around us can easily feel ignored, non-existent or mistreated when we focus on this journey we have embarked upon. That is a very dire mistake for they are the reason for all of this. Yes, it is wonderful that we will evolve and grow spiritually, but our mission is to better humanity. To leave this incarnation having made a positive impact on this planet and those who live here, especially those who are closest to us.

As we heal ourselves through our practice, extend that to those around you. Do not allow disagreements and old wounds to fester while you are trying to achieve more vaulted states of consciousness, for those old wounds will be like an anchor holding you back. This is especially true with family.

I know how difficult family can be, as they often are the ones that see our flaws most acutely and are proud to point them out to us. I do not take criticism well, and family is usually the first to speak out when things are not going my way. However, they can also be our greatest supporters.

Over the years, I have spoken with friends at length about familial difficulties. I have always urged them to take the high ground and make amends, no matter how insurmountable it may seem. Everyone, even those who criticize, struggle in day-to-day endeavors, and it is this common ground we must seek to overcome the chasms between us.

This applies to strife in all relationships. We cannot stand aloof to the needs of those around us when we have the power of the Divine within. Our practice and relationship with the Divine is what makes us powerful negotiators who can forge new relationships and repair dysfunctional ones.

I am not asking you to go out and re-build all the bridges that have been torn down throughout your life, but for those people who have been the closest to you throughout the years, you cannot let them go leaving nothing but open wounds in both. It will eat at you and surface in your practice as you relive many of life's poor choices and experiences. Heal them and you will heal you.

I have a very close friend whom I love dearly, and at the end of his first marriage, the marital strife between them caused a fracture between him and one of his children. At the time of this writing, they are still not communicating, and it hurts me to know they may never reconcile.

I have vowed to heal that fissure between them, but it will take time and probably more resources than I can bring to bear. I have set a seed within one of my daughters who may play a role in this down the road.

Though this does not directly affect me, knowing what I do about how important it is to heal such relationships, I cannot stand by while a good friend and his child suffer through this lifetime needlessly. As you grow in your practice, you may experience something similar.

Now, it is not our mission to heal every difficult relationship we hear about, and I will be the first to say it may not always be possible, but what servant of the Creator would not at least try if they thought it was in their power to help?

First, we must get our own house in order. Heal the wounds between you and your family and those around you who were pivotal in your life. It will heal both of you and your spiritual practice will jettison that anchor which holds you back. We must live and act as examples to all around us that living within our practice is powerful medicine.

The Next Level

You have reached the top of this practice for now, but as I mentioned earlier, there is more to come. Though I talked about a couple of these already, I wanted to list out some things which will eventually be released in future books:

- Lucid Serpent,
- Serpent Lightning,

- Serpent Abundance,
- Healing Serpent,
- Serpent Pyramid,
- The Emergence, and
- The Trial.

There will be higher levels coming in the future that will contain these new techniques. Lucid Serpent is a technique currently under development, and I honestly can't say how long it might take to fully develop. Working with my spirit guide, I feel confident I will soon be able to reveal the technique to the world.

Serpent Lightning was taught to me a while ago, but I have put it on the back burner because I feel it is almost too powerful at this stage. However, I asked for it and received it, so it is a technique that will have its time. I see myself using it to assist me with some other spiritual activities, including Lucid Serpent, so I will have much to say about this technique once I have more experience.

Serpent abundance is all about bringing more into your life and how that will change you and change how you deal with the world. Abundance is not a bad thing, but it can become a bad thing if it becomes an obsession. Work on your purpose and natural abundance will come your way for now. But later, I want the new humans to experience all that life offers as they move into a position of role model for other humans to emulate. It is best to cultivate wisdom before you gain abundance.

Healing is self-explanatory, and there will be plenty of healing during your Kriya Serpent Yoga practice. But what if we want to heal others? What if we want to teach others how to heal themselves? It is possible, and I will keep that at the top of my list, along with the other new techniques.

This practice will evolve, and I look to you to help make that happen. We live in very exciting times, and we have a very exciting future to look forward to despite the current chaos surrounding us. As we advance in our spiritual growth, we will become the vanguard of a new wave of humanity that will affect everything.

Welcome, new human. I am glad you have awakened.

Chapter 10

After Kriya Practice, sit long in meditation with attention fixed at Kutastha (the Spiritual Eye). The Soul-consciousness that usually flows outward into body-consciousness is turned inwardly by Kriya. Then the mind, freed from its attraction to external objects, will experience the wondrous inner world of Spirit.
Paramahansa Yogananda

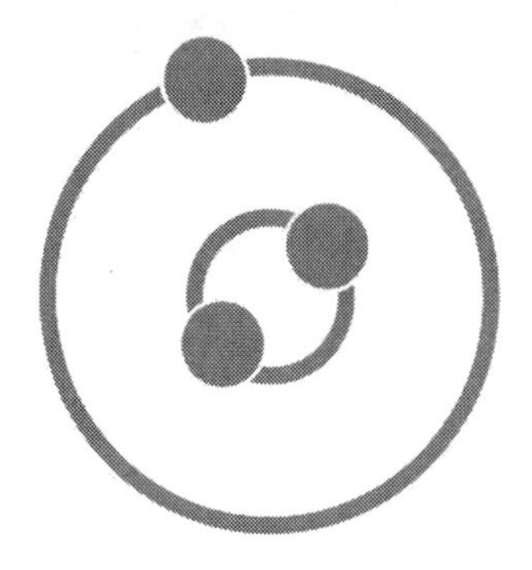

Effects of Kriya Serpent Yoga

This practice will change you in more ways than I can list in this book. However, the most profound will be the ongoing connection with the Divine and the relationship and knowledge such a connection will afford you. In the quote above, Paramahansa Yogananda says the "wondrous inner world of Spirit." He is referring to that connection with the Divine.

I spoke at some length about many of the effects you may experience, and they will be amazing, though sometimes scary. It is integral to any adventure, and we must embrace it as another gift for our spiritual awakening. Experience and emotions are a critical part of this evolutionary path.

I experience new things daily. Sometimes it is something new and amazing while meditating. Sometimes it is a new way to look at things while barely awake, lying in bed. Other times, it is a vision or fantastic insight or idea into my purpose, my life, or my spiritual knowledge while at work. Either way, it is a daily occurrence.

There was a time when the learning and experiences of my spiritual practice overwhelmed me during a period where my work life was killing me. I pleaded to the Divine for a break. A friend suggested I stop my daily regimen to take a break, and I did for a short while.

But that was only part of the equation. My plea was heard and everything within my practice temporarily ceased. It was a much deserved pit stop along my spiritual path. Do not be afraid if you need a break from time to time because this can be really heavy stuff.

This practice differs from standardized religion. I do not lecture on things you cannot see or experience for yourself. I don't ask for money in a tithing basket, sending you back to your deluded life of illusion, where you are disconnected from the powers that created you. In this practice, you will *see* and *experience* the truth of reality.

This is a dynamic and living process—always changing, always evolving while you grow. When I say it is like "I am" as Matias De Stefano says, I mean you will realize you are an integral part of this Universe and will sit in silent awe of what you *see* and *experience*.

This practice creates tangible changes in your psychological and physical health, preparing you to be an emissary of the Divine on earth. It will provide you with purpose, with love and compassion and a view of all the reality that was hidden from you.

You cannot get all that from a book! Only through experience can you truly transform, and this practice will provide you with all the experiences your Soul desires. You will become part of the enlightened cadre who will transform this world and all those who call it home. A home we all deserve and truly desire when we seriously look deep into our Soul.

As we practice, we will light up with the power of our Soul like a beacon for others to follow. As more of us awaken, we will unite as a network, chasing away the darkness of this current world, replacing it with the light of Divinity. We will use this network to drive the transformation of everything.

Our spiritual growth will eventually mirror our technological growth, and we will expand and wield that technology using true wisdom. For wisdom will be a hallmark of our practice. We will tap into the wisdom we have gained over many lifetimes and the wisdom of the Divine. You will gain wisdom beyond your years.

For me, one of my favorite effects is the clarity it has brought into my life. Indecision, fear, frustration and anger have all been removed from the major parts of my life. Oh sure, I still get riled when I am cutoff on the roadway, but I no longer wonder who I am or where I am going. You will see your life and all things within it with a clarity you may never have experienced before.

I have learned to change all experiences, whether good or bad, into something good. Buddha said the world we experience is the world we make, not the world others make for us. I don't blame others for my misfortunes because I am in charge of my life and my reality. This is a simple yet very powerful concept.

While you pursue your purpose, your continuing education will bring about a gestalt of significant import. You will finally see the world and reality for what it is: an illusion to control us and keep the Universal neighborhood hidden. Once you have that breakthrough, the Universe is literally the limit.

This will bring newfound intuition and you will see beyond the veil that hides so much from you. You will read the proverbial tea leaves and see the paths that are being charted without you. And you will take back that control and eventually free others from the same illusion.

However, conditioning is strong, and your ego will fight back. The "rational" ego will constantly battle you and try to convince you that the veil you have removed is a necessary part of who you are and who you must be. But as you further separate the real you from your ego, its power will fade into the background, freeing you to pursue your real purpose.

I have often talked about compassion, but what does that really mean? Universal love is something we all talk about, but is it something we can all have in our daily lives? When others come to us demanding we follow or else, can we stand strong and still love them? Do we want all to be free of the illusion? Should we free them all, or be like others through the centuries who kept secrets and never revealed the illusion to the common folk?

These are the emotional dramas that will plague us, but our practice will help us cultivate that true Universal love. You cannot feel the unconditional love of the Divine and then turn around and hate others who disagree with you. If the Divine loves everyone no matter what their course, then we must also love everyone, no matter their course.

This will manifest as a need to sit and speak to those with whom you disagree. Are you able to listen to them? Can you stand being in their company? Can you even remotely understand them and what motivates their beliefs? This is where that gestalt will come in handy. You are truly advanced when you get to this point.

When you finally understand the illusion of this world, then you will understand the motivation of those who wish it to remain within the illusion. Can you hate them for being programmed? Is it their fault they do not see the veil hiding the truth from them? Do you think the Divine hates them for that? The Divine doesn't hate them, and neither should you.

They all have the same potential we do, but not all have the same opportunity to live up to that potential. We will help change that and transform many more. I cannot hate any of them, not even those with the most egregious sins in their past, for inside them lives the Divine as inside us. They are deluded by the web of lies that have been erected around this world and all of us.

You will eventually experience true Universal love, and will use it with all people you meet, human or not. Never forget that everything you see is part of the Universe and the Creator. None has more rights than any other to the treasures within this Universe given to us as a gift of love. You extend that gift of love to all.

With the wisdom you cultivate through Kriya Serpent Yoga, you will move up in your worldly duties. That wisdom will open doors you never imagined possible. For every gift you receive, use your wisdom to use the gift for the greater good. You will still benefit but will expand the impact of that gift further beyond your own orbit.

If you live in a small world now, this practice will make you a world citizen, your reach extending far beyond the borders of your own country. Labels like ethnicity, citizenship and race will fade into the background as you realize we are all brothers and sisters. The discrimination leveled at those who are younger or older will disappear as you realize we are all on different parts of our journey no matter our age. We really are all the same.

Over time, your habits will change as you realize you no longer need the crutches that once kept your ego propped up. You will still enjoy life, in fact even more than you had before, because now you will see everything in a beautiful new light with attentive, fresh eyes and vision. I laugh more and more at people's behaviors as I realize the effects their path has on them.

You will experience all senses in a way you hadn't before, and you will eschew all things that impede this new sense of the material world. Clouding your mind with drugs and alcohol will seem ridiculous once you reach that new clarity of thought and live in the presence of the Divine.

You will not lose your sense of humor, but you will probably develop even more when you fully recognize the world around you. I sometimes laugh at the most mundane things as my mind spins fantastic tales about how they affect us and the world. There is so much humor in this world, embrace it and laugh. And you will learn to laugh at yourself as the practice lowers the pretentious barriers your ego has erected around you.

You will be freed from social stigma and social fear, free to express yourself in ways you would never have dreamed of before Kriya Serpent Yoga. So many of the social constructs built within this world are but tools of control, and you will be free from such controls. Eventually, you will show others how to free themselves from such constructs. Once they are free from the prison, they will never return, and they will grow and evolve.

For new humans, the manifestation of psychic abilities may be unsettling at first, though ultimately liberating. Each generation will manifest these powers more significantly than the prior generations. Part of the Kriya Serpent Yogi mandate is to prepare humanity for these revelations so science will embrace it and integrate it into society.

The new humans will need guidance, training and wisdom to wield these gifts, and Kriya Serpent Yoga will provide a framework to begin that process. Like wielding new technology, new powers will be difficult to master and use responsibly. We will be the teachers of the wisdom to make that happen. As your gifts manifest, seek that internal wisdom and use your gifts for the good of humanity and your purpose. You will be called upon someday to help teach others that wisdom.

Once you fully experience the gestalt I mentioned earlier, you will see all the cracks in this world. Kriya Serpent Yoga practice will show you how to fill those cracks and fix everything that is broken. As I mentioned before, the new age will be a time of healing and revelations. Many of those revelations will begin within you during your practice, so be prepared and write everything down.

That is why I speak of seeing with fresh eyes. The wisdom you gain will manifest in ideas and knowledge you can apply to our world. Remember, the new humans will be architects and builders of this new world, and there lies your purpose. Can you imagine a world without all the troubles of today? I can, and so will you.

Though I have yet to mention this, there are ancient organizations that have played a role in humanity's evolution over thousands of years. These organizations will soon reveal themselves, and we will work with them to create our enlightened world. They will bring knowledge, wisdom and resources to assist us during this new age.

Eventually, we will work hand in hand with Galactic neighbors to build this world anew. Kriya Serpent Yoga practitioners will be on the ground floor of this new era of unprecedented cooperation, and our purpose will be supported by their wisdom, knowledge and resources. The pages of science fiction will soon play out within our world, and you will be there to greet it with wisdom and love.

The more you practice, the more you'll rebuild all aspects of yourself, realizing the beautiful Soul that has been kept hidden by your ego. Using your memories of past lives, you will integrate their wisdom into your daily life, and transform on all levels. You will leave the scared child behind and embrace the ancient Soul you are.

Your evolution has brought you into this world during a time of incredible revelations. You will soon clear a path for the world we have all imagined. Relish in this remarkable and fantastic time, for your role within it is a miracle of the Divine. All your past lives prepared you for this incarnation, and now that the time has arrived, you can live like no prior incarnation.

The power of Kundalini will charge you so that any obstacle will be as flimsy as the veil that places them before you. You will say "I can" and deliver on that promise. No more doubts will plague your every step, and you will see far beyond those around you who have yet to awaken. You will finally be the change you want to see in this world.

If you have a partner, share the path with them and you will discover a relationship that will blossom with untold beauty and love. To share the most intimate of our internal thoughts with another without fear of ment or rejection is something we have all craved but few dare to explore. Once all is laid bare by your practice, you will be liberated from your past and can move forward with your partner anew. I wish my wife had survived to see this, but my new partner is just as wonderful and fully engaged in our spiritual growth.

As the real you emerges from within, keep in mind the following things to aid in this metamorphosis. These will be pivotal to your final transformation, so continue your efforts in each of these areas.

Education

We are given a brain to think, but we cannot think correctly without training our brains first. Education is not just a right, but a mandatory exercise to assist us in using the tools the Divine has given us. That is why education was kept secret for thousands of years. It was power and only divvied out to a select few dedicated enough to be chosen.

It is ironic today that one of the most powerful things in humanity is now considered useless by the cultural norms sweeping around the world. While there may be many reasons for this failure in education, followers of Kriya Serpent Yoga will not abandon it. You must always be learning, both in the material world and in the spiritual world. Without that, it is the equivalent of going into a modern battlefield with nothing but a sword. The machine guns, missiles and bombs will obliterate you from the earth.

Here is where advice is important. If you did not get a college degree, do not fret because you can still pursue knowledge online, often at a vastly reduced cost or for free. But what should you study? Anything related to your purpose and your life. How can you achieve your purpose if you know nothing about it? I had to form a non-profit, but knew nothing about it. So I went out and learned, consuming as much information as I could from the Internet, books and people.

Humanity is on the verge of merging spiritual practice with science, as it was long ago. When that happens, a new frontier of technology will manifest. We will need this technology to lead us into the Cosmos to join our brothers and sisters that live among the stars.

If you are like me and want to pursue becoming a mystic, there are ways to make that happen. Refer to the *Resources* chapter at the end of this book and see the organizations where you can learn mysticism. I am a member of one of them, but all are working towards the same ends. One may call to you, so check them out.

Education is a fundamental part of your life, your purpose and your evolutionary journey. You should always put time aside for your educational pursuits. If not, you will be like the rock that dreams of being a magnificent sculpture. You will never smooth your rough edges nor form that new image of yourself without education. It hones us, chiseling away at our rough exteriors and polishing us into the perfect being we can be.

Begin your lifelong passion for learning, for it is the water upon which your evolution thrives. As you learn and grow, an amazing Universe will unfold before you, and you will become more than you ever imagined you could be. There is magic in this Universe, go find it.

Fitness

You do not have to be Arnold Schwarzenegger to enjoy the benefits of Kriya Serpent Yoga, but a positive life state is required for full benefits. Physical fitness is part of a positive life state. Don't spend thousands to be the next physical fitness guru, but prepare a thoughtful plan to integrate physical fitness into your weekly lifestyle.

Our bodies are instruments, and fine tuning them makes our practice better. Even the best online gamers typically have a regular fitness routine to make them capable of the rigorous gaming for hours on end. Fitness is a necessity.

As a new human, you will enjoy a long lifetime. While my generation has enjoyed lifetimes in their eighties and nineties, new humans should easily add ten to twenty years onto that. As our technology evolves, the medical miracles of today will be common practice tomorrow.

Cancer, heart disease, dementia and other chronic illnesses will soon be a thing of the past. It will happen within your lifetime, so buckle in because you have a lot of years ahead.

When practicing Kriya Serpent Yoga, enjoy life to the fullest and pursue your purpose. These will fulfill you during your long life. I cannot express how beautiful and miraculous life really is. Once you travel a short distance down your spiritual path, you will understand what I am talking about.

People often fear getting old, and the number one complaint is losing their ability to fully enjoy life because of chronic illness and a degraded physical state. *Aging will kill you!* That was how it was designed. But did you ever ask how it does so?

Over time, DNA is damaged through environmental conditions such as radiation, oxidation within the body and toxic substances introduced into our systems. As the DNA degrades, errors in the sequences are passed on to new cells through cellular division. Therefore, these errors propagate into new cells, further degrading our life conditions.

There are ways to minimize this degradation. Some people have natural immunity to aging as their bodies possess natural defenses against the environmental conditions. These same people usually have natural immunities to chronic conditions such as cancer. I have some of that protection handed down by relatives who lived long and prosperous lives.

Today, you don't just have to be blessed with innate protection passed down through generations. There are plenty of ways to keep a healthy body over time, and number one is physical fitness. Number two is a nutritional diet.

My physical appearance shows the power of fitness, as I am often mistaken for being decades younger than I am. However, time is catching up, and some of the hallmark signs of age have reversed that. However, physically, I am easily as fit as someone ten to twenty years younger than me. My lifetime fitness regimen has given me a positive life state that is far younger than most people my age. You can enjoy these same benefits.

I am not here to discuss or teach you the physical aspects of yoga because I do not need to. You can find a wealth of information on this topic all over the Internet. I strongly urge you to seek them out and begin with simple techniques. Even as little as ten minutes a day of light, physical yoga can have a very beneficial effect on your life state and your Kriya Serpent practice.

Walking, biking, running, sports, weights, aerobics, Pilates and more than I can list are all out there waiting for you to try them and see which one fits your lifestyle and your preferences. Each body is different and will respond to different exercise in different ways. You must explore which fits you best, then stick with it forever.

Doesn't mean you need only do one thing, but that is the minimum. Here is a list of what I do regularly:

- weightlifting,
- biking,
- pickleball,
- golf, and
- kayaking.

Obviously, some of these are too time intensive to do all the time, but I fit them in because they make me feel better and they are fun. Weightlifting has been a regular weekly practice for me for much of my life, and I still have a rigorous regimen I follow to maintain muscle and overall fitness. Yes, you lose muscle over time if you do not exercise. That process starts around your mid to late thirties and continues until you die, but you can slow that process.

One aspect of fitness many overlook is the connection to a strong and positive mental state. Eliminate stress, chronic illness and a low energy life state and you will see an immediate increase in your mental state. It may not eliminate your anxiety and depression, but it will significantly reduce their effects on you. It has worked for me my whole life.

I have resources available in the last chapter of this book that will help you start your physical fitness journey or improve it if you already have a routine. No matter how old or young you are, you must continue to exercise to be the best you can to support your spiritual journey. Your body is the instrument of all you do. Take care of it as though it is the most precious thing you have because it is.

Sexuality

This is a loaded topic depending on which culture you come from. The world contains everything from promiscuity to chastity and all things in between. In many societies, sexuality is viewed as taboo or inherently evil, while others celebrate it as an amazing gift of life to be fully enjoyed.

I am not here to tell which side of the coin you should be on in relation to sexuality. However, it is a fundamental aspect of life (it is how life emerges), so we must touch upon it. After all, if you are just starting down your spiritual path, you need guidance on this topic.

As stated throughout, you want a positive life state so that you can fully benefit from the Kriya Serpent Yoga practice. Sexuality is part of that positive life state. Is it evil? No. Is it dangerous? Maybe. Should we fully embrace it or shun it as we attempt to achieve spiritual enlightenment? Depends.

Paramahansa Yogananda wrote in his autobiography that sexual relations between partners were best enjoyed no more than once or twice a month. I know for some, you might question that. You are conditioned to enjoy sexual relations many times a week, so the idea of once or twice a month seems impossible. For others, monthly seems excessive. We must all recognize we are in different places on this spectrum and respect that fact.

Remember, you are a combination of not just your current life, but many lifetimes before this. In those previous lifetimes, you may have enjoyed sex like it was going out of style, and in this lifetime, you are less interested. There is nothing wrong with this. Experiences are why we are here, and sexuality is an experience.

Let's start from the beginning and then you can judge where you are with all of this. First, if you have not done so, you need to learn more about human sexuality. *No, I don't mean through practice!* Search out and find all the latest scientific information you can on human sexuality. How can you have a healthy relationship with your sexuality when you don't even know what it is?

I took a course called *Human Sexuality* in college. I was already interested in human psychology, and sexuality seemed like a major driver of human behavior, so I took the course. It was fantastic, and I learned an enormous amount. Make yourself smart about what it is and what it isn't before exploring the practice of it.

Yes, we all have the feelings, but we need not act out on them without first understanding them. This is a gross omission from our education system that is often based on fear, ancient dogmas and outright incorrect information. We are biological creatures and sex is a biological process, so we should all know whatever we can about it before we make mandates and decisions about it. Ignorance has been the problem for too long.

Now, critics will assume I am promoting a sex cult or some such ridiculous claim. They search for demons everywhere, especially if it is something new. I promote a healthy life state and knowledge. Sex, like anything else, can be horribly abused with awful consequences, and I am not about that. I don't want anyone to overeat, drink, exercise, have sex, or anything else that becomes obsessive. Seek only worldly pleasures and you will not find happiness.

In fact, I see both paths having profound implications. Promiscuity and chastity can offer unique opportunities to experience life and enhance spirituality. Sexuality is a gift from the Divine, and that energy can be harnessed to achieve transcendental states or cause psychological harm.

Both abstinence and plenty can be fruitful, but excess can lead to obsession, which lowers your life state. It comes down to you, but knowledge is critical. View sexuality as you do anything else, with the wisdom and intelligence given to us by the Divine.

You can make sex a positive part of your spiritual journey and you can make it a hindrance to your evolution. Your decisions will determine which it will be. Our species has an underlying imperative to reproduce, and that life-force (Kundalini) is an integral part of our practice. Therefore, sexuality may be unfairly associated with our yoga.

Kundalini can cause sexual feelings, sometimes intense. However, we are intelligent enough to harness that power for spiritual good and not just for a "good time." That energy is essential to life, so do not waste it on short-term thrills. Learn to channel it into your spiritual evolution. Enjoy sex, but do it responsibly and not automatically.

Some of the Tantric techniques teach us how to harness that energy without the release of the energy that often lowers our vibrational state. Therefore, you can eat your cake and have it too. I have practiced such things myself, and found it was another great way to tap into my Kundalini. But be careful, it could easily lead to obsession.

I caution that anything that can bring such pleasure has the potential to cause addiction. Therefore, I urge you to consider not traveling down that path until you have achieved some measure of spiritual growth first. And if you wish to travel down that path with a partner, be certain they have also attained that same spiritual maturity.

Though I feel like I do not need to say this, I will anyway. No matter what path you choose for your sexuality, please ensure that you have full consent of any partner, and that whatever actions you pursue are for love and spiritual growth. There are great resources on this topic that I have included in the last chapter of this book. Do research before you dive into anything.

Sexuality IS NOT part of the Kriya Serpent Yoga practice.

Though Kriya Serpent Yoga can enhance your sexuality through Kundalini, it is not the reason we practice. It should never be used to mislead others under the guise of spiritual enlightenment. For most, spiritual enlightenment is best achieved *without sexual practices.*

Habits

I touched upon these earlier, but I think it best to address them again, as so many in this world suffer from them. Some habits are good (Kriya Serpent Yoga) while others can be detrimental to our health and our spirituality. Our health is obvious, but our spirituality may be less so.

I have talked about love, clarity and a positive life state through our practice. If Universal love is an important attainment for your purpose, then anything interfering with that could prevent you from realizing your potential. Bad habits are typically a selfish, self-absorbent act to distract us from the perceived hardships of life.

I truly understand. I had my selfish addictions during this life, but put them all to rest. It was difficult, and yes, I still think about them regularly. As I transformed, like Paramahansa Yogananda promised, I found my body and mind no longer needed or wanted that distraction from reality. That is what they are, distractions from our everyday hardships.

I am not urging you to go out and join Alcoholics Anonymous, or any other addiction organization, but if you continue down this path, you will want to shed your addictions. If they are too strong to overcome by yourself, reach out to whatever is available to help you beat it.

To quit smoking cigarettes, I had to use nicotine gum. I wasn't even that big a smoker, but the nicotine was too powerful for me to overcome on my own. This was long before my current practice. Kriya Serpent Yoga will help, but may not help completely if the drug of choice is powerful and your addiction has gone on for a long time.

Use your newfound strength and resolve to seek help and break the habit once and for all. You will never regret it and it will transform you more than you can even imagine right now. After a lifetime of drinking, I can sit comfortably in a bar or party without even the slightest desire for a drink. I still love the smell of smoking and miss it, but there is no longer a craving.

I also mentioned food as an addiction, and that is quite real. The joke in my family was if you wanted to find one of us, go to where the food is. My father remembered travel destinations for the food he ate there. He had an unhealthy relationship with food most of his life.

I love food like my father did, but learned it can be an addiction. Even though I have tried to cultivate a healthy relationship with food, I often fall short of a healthy diet. Time and a hectic lifestyle are to blame for my lack of conscious eating. I still love many things that are not good for me, so it is hard to give them all up.

My savior has been exercise. Keeping the weight off and raising my overall life state has enabled me to cut away many of the poor diet choices I used to have and steered me towards the healthier end of the spectrum. There is still room for me to grow in this area. I am sure many of you could also grow more in your healthy diets.

Start small. Give up a single habitual treat you know is not good for you. It will be hard at first, but over time, you will feel better. As you practice Kriya Serpent Yoga, you find that your body will crave healthier choices. It will be subtle at first, but overtime it can become habitual, and that is when the true positive life state can fully emerge.

Regardless of your bad habits, do not beat yourself up for them. We have all had them or still have them, but with Kriya Serpent Yoga, you will see them as the crutch they are. As you work on the transformation through your practice, your desire will diminish. Your body naturally wants a healthy, positive life state, but our egos usually crush it as it tries to deal with stress, traumas and self-image. That will change.

Welcome New Humans

I started this book welcoming new humans and will end it the same way. Humanity is on the verge of something quite incredible and the new humans are the ones who will help usher in that incredible new age. This practice was given to me as a gift for all the new humans, hoping it would awaken them to their true nature and purpose.

If you have begun this practice and are being transformed by it, then welcome new human. The Divine is entrusting you with the keys to humanity's future. Use them well, and we will see miracles spread across this planet. This is a time of revelations and a time of healing, and you are the ones who will help bring about each.

Relish your new role, build a positive life state and show others what this practice can do for them. Once you see beyond the veil that hides the Universe from you, you will be forever changed. It is wondrous and truly magical; a Universe of immense beauty and love. Bring to this Universe the gifts you have been endowed with and you will be welcomed as the brother and sister you are.

Everything we experience is a creation of the Divine, and within each of us is a fractional part of that Divine. Embrace it and learn from it. It will carry you through countless lifetimes, bringing with it a bounty of experiences and wisdom you can apply in all incarnations. That first step in your spiritual awakening and journey is yours to take.

Don't have an ordinary life, but an extraordinary one. See the true reality currently beyond your basic senses. Though I cannot promise you will have every experience I have, you will gain so much more than you have right now. You will know truth, love and everlasting peace, conquering your fears of death, while eliminating self-doubt. Emerge from this practice as an enlightened being.

I hope you take that first step and join us in an opportunity of many lifetimes. *Welcome, new human!*

Resources

The following is a list of the resources to help with your spiritual journey in this practice. Be aware, the Internet is an ever-changing place, and any links listed below may no longer be valid. However, a simple search on the keywords for the item you are interested in should yield the results you need. Other than the One Minute Mystic, my commercial venture, I do not have any relationships with these other resources at the time of publishing and recommend them only based on my own personal experiences.

One Minute Mystic

This is the home of Kriya Serpent Yoga and you can get there by the various links listed below. I have also listed contact information so that you can join the community of practitioners and keep up to date on the all the latest Kriya Serpent news:

- Home for Kriya Serpent Yoga:
  www.OneMinuteMystic.com
- Me and my partner's esoteric blog/podcast:
  www.Childzero.com
- Non-profit dedicated to my purpose:
  www.InstituteForHumanEvolution.org
- Non-profit dedicated to my purpose:
  www.GlobalManifestProject.org

Kriya Serpent Supplies

I do not have any business relationship with the companies listed below unless stated clearly in the description. However, I have found them to be reputable, carry good products, and offer good customer service. Please use any companies you deem best for your needs:

www.DharmaCrafts.com—Great place for quality supplies but a bit pricier.

www.DharmaShop.com—Quality supplies, especially Mala Beads.

www.BareFootNative.com—Local shop for crystals you can order online.

www.Etsy.com—Various handmade things from this online marketplace.

Kriya Yoga

As I mentioned in this book, I am a big fan of two of the Kriya Yoga teachers listed below, but there are far more resources. I have listed more resources, some of which they refer to in their own literature. All of them I have accessed and used, so I have listed them because I believe they are valuable for your continuing education.

While I am no longer a member of the Self Realization Fellowship (SRF), I have added them to the list because of their wonderful beginning program. As I mentioned before, it is a year-long course designed and written by Paramahansa Yogananda himself, and is well worth considering if you are new. Check it out and see if it fits with your spiritual aspirations. It would be complementary to Kriya Serpent Yoga, like a Level 0, and you will learn a lot.

I have listed Paramahansa Yogananda's autobiography first because it is what started it all here in the West. It was my inspiration and will be yours too. Enjoy these resources and learn from them:

- *Autobiography of a Yogi* by Paramahansa Yogananda. This is where the magic started for me and my practice.
- Self-Realization Fellowship—Paramahansa Yogananda's organization for Kriya Yoga.

- SantataGamana—Author of the *Kriya Yoga Exposed* book among others.
- Kriya Yoga International—Organization that promotes Kriya Yoga.
- Yogoda Satsanga Society of India—Another of Paramahansa Yogananda's organizations.
- *Kriya Secrets Revealed* by J.C. Stevens. Teaches Kriya Yoga.

Mystery Schools

While no one needs to become a mystic to pursue their purpose, it provides a great deal of tools to help you along your spiritual journey. Their knowledge has been carried down through the ages and kept secret to all but those who decide to walk the path. I have enjoyed being a Rosicrucian over multiple lifetimes:

- www.rosicrucian.org—Ancient Mystical Order Rosae Crucis
- www.ModernMysterySchoolint.org—The Modern Mystery School
- www.BeAFreemason.org—Involved in the betterment of humanity and this world.
- www.KnightTemplar.org—Yes, they still exist, and are dedicated to Jesus.

Tantra

Tantric Yoga is really another means to achieve Kundalini, but it has been associated with the sexual practices that help to harness and focus that energy for spiritual purposes. Unfortunately, many only pursue it for the sexual pleasures rather than the spiritual growth of oneself or a couple. Go for the spiritual growth, and you will increase the sexual pleasure and enter into a state of bliss:

- *Tantra Exposed* by SantataGammana. Excellent book on the topic.
- *Tantra: The Art of Conscious Loving* by Caroline Muir and Charles Muir. For modern couples, this is the book for your spiritual growth.
- *Kundalini Tantra* by Swami Satyananda Saraswati. Another comprehensive book on Kundalini Tantric Yoga.

Fitness

Need to begin a fitness routine to help with your spiritual practice? These resources can help you whether you only want a simple routine or something much more. I have used them myself and highly recommend each one:

- Yoga with Kassandra—I love Kassandra's yoga routines, especially her 10-minute yoga.
- 10x Fitness—Got me in the best shape of my life with nothing more than 30-minute workouts at the gym 2 to 3 times a week.
- Pickleball—This is both fun and will get you in shape and let you meet new people. In many places, you can play for free in your local parks.
- eBikes—I love my eBike and can tell you it is far superior to a regular bike for ease of use while still getting exercise.

Education

There is a great deal of multimedia out there that offers aspiring spiritual mystics an enormous set of resources for their continuing education:

- Gaia—Member Supported Network which is an incredible place to start your journey into the spiritual and mystical reality that we all live within.

- Mindvalley—Member Supported Network similar to Gaia. A fantastic place to explore meditation and all types of self-help methodologies to take you spiritually, physically and mentally to the highest life state possible.
- MUFON—The Mutual UFO Network is based in Cincinnati, Ohio, and has been around for quite some time. They are the leading experts on all things related to Unidentified Flying Objects, or as the military now calls them, Unidentified Arial Phenomenon (UAPs).
- Sirius Disclosure—The CE-5 protocols are a very important topic for all practitioners of Kriya Serpent Yoga. It is through our practice that we reach out to the intelligence that exists beyond our small planet, but it is the protocols outlined within the CE-5 program that help us be successful Ambassadors for Humanity.
- Ancient Aliens—History Channel's show that picks up where Erich von Daniken left off. You often get a lot of snickers when you mention the show, but I have to tell you, through my practice I have had a gestalt from what this show brings to us coupled with my own experiences and those of associates that made me realize a lot of what they reveal is true.
- Monroe Institute—Using multiple methodologies to develop your psychic abilities. I use the Monroe Institute's Expand meditation app which uses special frequencies like binaural beats to entrain the brain into specific states of consciousness. I use it as an adjunct expansion to my work with Kriya Serpent Yoga.
- Noetic Sciences—Scientific studies of psychic phenomenon. This institute was founded by Dr. Edgar Mitchell, an Apollo 14 astronaut. His profound experience while on his moon mission turned him towards the science and experience of our psychic selves.

- Fundacion Arsayian—Started by Matias De Stefano and not affiliated with our institute (yet), they are directly working on bringing the new age to life to rebuild the world we live in.
- 4biddenKnowledge—Billy Carson is one of the most knowledgeable people on earth today about our true ancient history. Learn about your past to learn about your future.

Books

I have read all these books and recommend them for an overview of multiple topics to get you started on your journey:

- *Modern Buddhism* by Geshe Kelsang Gyatso. A good introductory book on Buddhism.
- *Conversations with God* by Neale Donald Walsch. *Speaking with the Divine*. Excellent.
- *Real Magic* by Dean I. Radin. Ancient Wisdom, Modern Science and a Guide to the Secret Power of the Universe.
- *Tell Me What You See* by Edward A. Dames. A true book on the use of Remote Viewing by US Military Intelligence. A friend of mine was trained by him.
- *Indigo Adults* by Kabir Jaffe. Great explanations for those new humans who are grown up.
- *BEQOMING* by Azrya Bequer and Benjamin Bequer. A fabulous, inspirational book that my partner turned me on to. It is profound and will help you with your spiritual journey.

Specific Shows

These shows should at least pique your curiosity and perhaps convince you there is more to reality than you thought, so maybe Kriya Serpent Yoga is worth exploring to lead you to even more revelations:

- *Kundalini*—Great overview of Kundalini. Note, Kriya Serpent Yoga will achieve Kundalini quickly for all new humans.
- *The Journey of Remembering*—Once you remember your past lives, you will change in a most profound way like Matias De Stefano.
- *Transcendance & the Pineal*—Connections between Kundalini and transcendent states of consciousness.
- *Close Encounters of the 5th Kind: Origins*—Find out how it started.
- *Third Eye Spies*—I wonder why the government brushes off psychic phenomenon while they actively use it.
- *Samadhi: Maya: The Illusion of Self – Fully understanding who you are*. Watch all episodes of this series.
- *The 900-Year Secret of the Knights Templar*—Mysteries deepen... but these were mystical knights who knew the truth.
- *Insider Secrets of the Knights Templar*—I realize most will not take my word on this, but what he is talking about in this interview is quite real. I have sources.
- *Transcending the Biblical Narrative*—Much truth in these revelations. Most of us have been programmed by the churches that still rule spirituality on this world.
- *Ancient Apocalypse*—If you want an enlightening introduction to the real history of our world, this show will open your eyes to an alternative timeline that defies traditional thinking.
- *Superhuman*—A great view into the psychic abilities all people have.
- *AWARE*—A great scientific and spiritual look at consciousness. Without consciousness, there would be no Universe.

- *Orion: Origin of the Gods*—Interesting connections between multiple megalithic sites around the world.

MANTRA
BOOKS

Recent bestsellers from MANTRA BOOKS are:

The Way Things Are

A Living Approach to Buddhism

Lama Ole Nydahl

An introduction to the teachings of the Buddha, and how to make use of these teachings in everyday life.

Paperback: 978-1-84694-042-2 ebook: 978-1-78099-845-9

Back to the Truth

5000 Years of Advaita

Dennis Waite

A demystifying guide to Advaita for both those new to, and those familiar with this ancient, non-dualist philosophy from India.

Paperback: 978-1-90504-761-1 ebook: 978-184694-624-0

Shinto: A celebration of Life

Aidan Rankin

Introducing a gentle but powerful spiritual pathway reconnecting humanity with Great Nature and affirming all aspects of life.

Paperback: 978-1-84694-438-3 ebook: 978-1-84694-738-4

In the Light of Meditation

Mike George

A comprehensive introduction to the practice of meditation and the spiritual principles behind it. A 10 lesson meditation programme with CD and internet support.

Paperback: 978-1-90381-661-5

A Path of Joy

Popping into Freedom

Paramananda Ishaya

A simple and joyful path to spiritual enlightenment.

Paperback: 978-1-78279-323-6 ebook: 978-1-78279-322-9

The Less Dust the More Trust
Participating in The Shamatha Project, Meditation and Science Adeline van Waning, MD PhD
The inside-story of a woman participating in frontline meditation research, exploring the interfaces of mind-practice, science and psychology.
Paperback: 978-1-78099-948-7 ebook: 978-1-78279-657-2

I Know How To Live, I Know How To Die
The Teachings of Dadi Janki: A warm, radical, and life-affirming view of who we are, where we come from, and what time is calling us to do
Neville Hodgkinson
Life and death are explored in the context of frontier science and deep soul awareness.
Paperback: 978-1-78535-013-9 ebook: 978-1-78535-014-6

Living Jainism
An Ethical Science
Aidan Rankin, Kanti V. Mardia
A radical new perspective on science rooted in intuitive awareness and deductive reasoning.
Paperback: 978-1-78099-912-8 ebook: 978-1-78099-911-1

Ordinary Women, Extraordinary Wisdom
The Feminine Face of Awakening
Rita Marie Robinson
A collection of intimate conversations with female spiritual teachers who live like ordinary women, but are engaged with their true natures.
Paperback: 978-1-84694-068-2 ebook: 978-1-78099-908-1

The Way of Nothing

Nothing in the Way

Paramananda Ishaya

A fresh and light-hearted exploration of the amazing reality of nothingness.

Paperback: 978-1-78279-307-6 ebook: 978-1-78099-840-4